Thirty MORE Days to MUSIC THEORY

Ready-to-use Lessons and Reproducible Activities For the Music Classroom

By Sharon Stosur

Table of Contents

ISBN 978-1-4234-1073-7

HAL•LEONARD® CORPORATION

7777 W. BLUEMOUND RD. P.O. BOX 13819 MILWAUKEE, WI 53213

BEAT AND RHYTHM

Name ____

Beat is a steady, recurring pulse. Musical beat can be easy to hear. It can be strong and accented, or gently repetitious. It can cause us to tap our toe or get up and dance! How many other types of beat can you identify in the world around you? List some examples below:

Beat you can produce with your body:	**Beat** created by technology:	**Beat** found in nature:
1. _________________	1. _________________	1. _________________
2. _________________	2. _________________	2. _________________
3. _________________	3. _________________	3. _________________

HEAR THE BEAT!

Sing or listen to a favorite song and feel the musical beat. How would you describe the beat? Write the name of the song below and circle all that apply. Add to the list if necessary.

Song Title:____

fast	regular	calm
slow	irregular	agitated
medium	accented	strong

Rhythm is a pattern of sound and silence with a beat; music is generally organized into rhythms that can be heard or felt.

FEEL THE BEAT!

Tap or clap each beat indicated by ❘. Listen carefully to keep the beat steady.

❘	❘	❘	❘	❘	❘	❘	❘

(beat)   (beat)   (beat)   etc.

Use ⅃ to indicate a beat of silence. Tap or clap only on the beats indicated by ❘. Say "sh" on the silent beats.

(beat)   (beat)   "sh"

STEADY YOURSELF

Practice keeping a steady beat using each example below. Try each example using a slow beat and then again with a faster beat. At any speed, the beat should remain steady.

1. | | ≀ | | ≀ | | ≀   ≀ | |

2. | ≀   ≀ | ≀   ≀ | ≀   ≀ | | |

3. | | | | ≀ | | | ≀ | | |

4. ≀ | ≀ | ≀ | ≀ | ≀   ≀ | |

PROJECT: WRITE YOUR OWN RAP!

Beat is a defining characteristic of many types of music. Marches have a strong **1**-2, **1**-2 feel. Waltzes have a strong beat 1 and gentler beats 2 and 3: **1**-2-3, **1**-2-3. In some types of modern music, the beat is unpredictable and unusual. Rap music uses a pulsating beat combined with spoken words that are accented and often rhyme.

Write a Rap about your pet or a favorite animal. Create four lines about your animal. You may wish to use pairs of rhyming lines as in the example below.

> My fluffy pet cat,
> He's really very fat,
> Sleepin' all day
> But that's okay.

Use the lines below to write your Rap.

____

____

____

____

After you've written your four lines, practice speaking the words aloud. Add a beat pattern by snapping, tapping, stomping or otherwise sounding your beat. Speak your lyrics over the beat pattern. Share your Rap with other classmates, teaching them the beat pattern so they can join you. Perform your Raps for the class.

CHALLENGE

Work with classmates to combine your beat patterns. Choose one Rap. Choose two students' beat patterns. Practice speaking the lyrics over both beat patterns at the same time. Experiment with different combinations of beat patterns to find the ones that you like the best. For more fun try adding a third beat pattern.

NOTES, RESTS AND VALUE

Name ____

Music is notated (written down) using **notes** and **rests**. Notes are symbols for sound, and rests are symbols for silence. Some common notes and rests include:

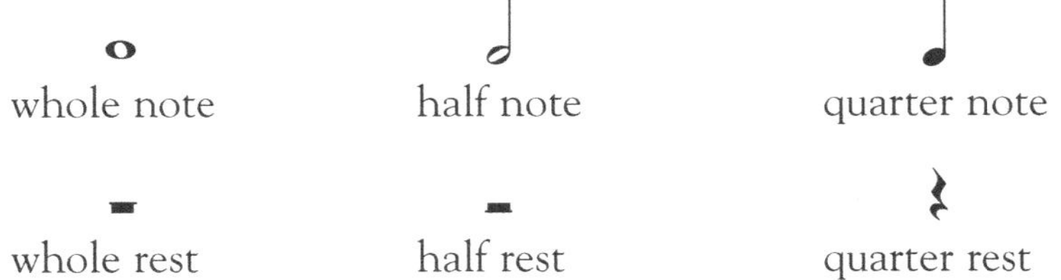

NOTATION PRACTICE

A **whole note** is drawn as an oval, and can be placed above, below or through the line. Draw seven more whole notes.

A **half note** looks like a whole note with a line added called a stem. Stems are drawn pointing up on the right side and pointing down on the left side of the note. Draw seven more half notes above, below or through the line.

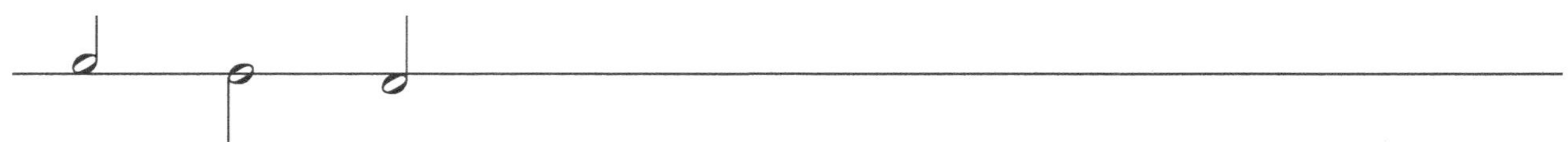

A **quarter note** looks like a half note with the note head filled in. Draw seven more quarter notes above, below or through the line.

Every note value in music has a corresponding **rest**.

Practice drawing rests above, below or through the line. Draw three more of each rest. Be sure to notice exactly where each part of the rest is placed relative to the line.

Value (also called duration) is how long a note sounds, or a silence lasts. Numbers are used to show the value.

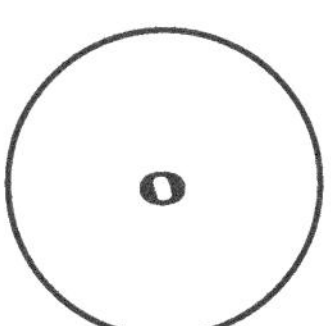

whole note

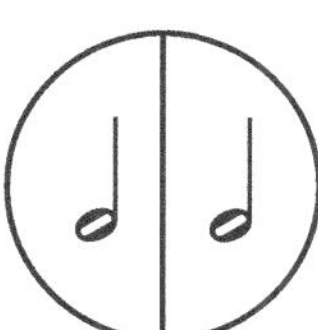

half note

quarter note

Quarter notes are often used as a unit of beat, or ♩ = 1 beat.

Half notes are twice as long as quarter notes, or 𝅗𝅥 = 2 beats.

Whole notes are twice as long as half notes, or 𝅝 = 4 beats.

♩ = 1 beat

𝅗𝅥 = 2 beats

𝅝 = 4 beats

MUSIC MATH

True or False?

1. T   F   𝅗𝅥 = 2 beats

2. T   F   ♩ = 4 beats

3. T   F   𝅝 = 4 beats

4. T   F   ♩ + ♩ + ♩ + ♩ = 4 beats

5. T   F   ♩ + 𝅗𝅥 + 𝅗𝅥 = 4 beats

6. T   F   𝅗𝅥 + 𝅗𝅥 = 4 beats

7. T   F   𝅗𝅥 + ♩ + 𝄽 = 4 beats

8. T   F   ▬ + ▬ = 4 beats

9. T   F   ♩ + ♩ + 𝅗𝅥 + 𝅗𝅥 = 4 beats

10. T   F   𝅝 + 𝅝 = 4 beats

Fill in the blank.

1. ♩ + ♩ = _______ beats

2. ♩ + ♩ = _______ beats

3. ♩ + ♩ + ♩ = _______ beats

4. o – ♩ = _______ beats

5. o + ♩ + ♩ = _______ beats

6. o – ♩ = _______ beats

7. ▬ – ♩ = _______ beats

8. o + ♩ + ▬ = _______ beats

9. ♩ + ♩ + o = _______ beats

10. o + o + ♩ = _______ beats

PROJECT: MUSIC MATH GENIUS

How many ways can you notate 16 beats? Use these note and rest values in any combination:

Here is a sample of one way to notate 16 beats:

o + ♩ + ♩ + ♩ + ▬ + ♩ + ♩ + o = 16 beats

Notate at least four more ways. Share your notations with the class by writing them on the board. How many different ways did you come up with as a class?

1. ____

2. ____

3. ____

4. ____

METER AND TIME SIGNATURE

Name _______________________________

Music is divided into sections by **bar lines**. The distance between two bar lines is called a **measure**. A **double bar line** comes at the end.

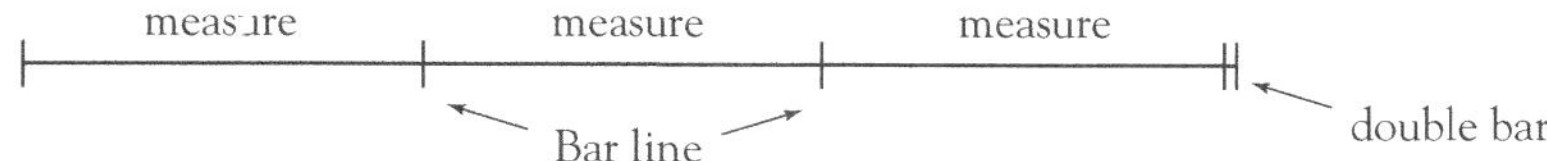

Meter is the number of beats in a measure. Numbers are used to organize meter. The number of beats in each measure is determined by the meter and indicated by a symbol called a **time signature**. Time signatures appear at the beginning of the music and use two numbers placed one above the other. The upper number indicates how many beats are in each measure. The lower number designates the note value that will receive one beat. Complete the chart below.

RHYTHM DIVISION

Divide the following rhythm patterns into measures. Be sure to notice the time signature for each example, and add a double bar at the end.

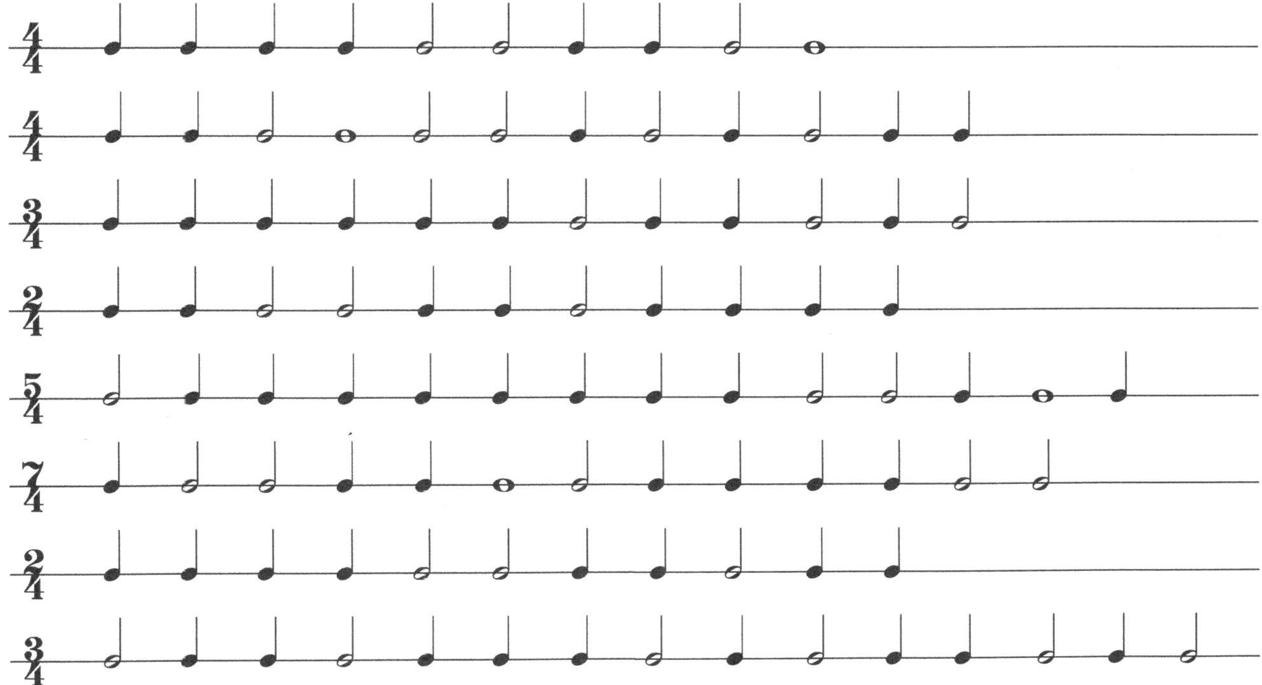

DO YOU HAVE THE TIME?

Add the correct time signature to each rhythm example below:

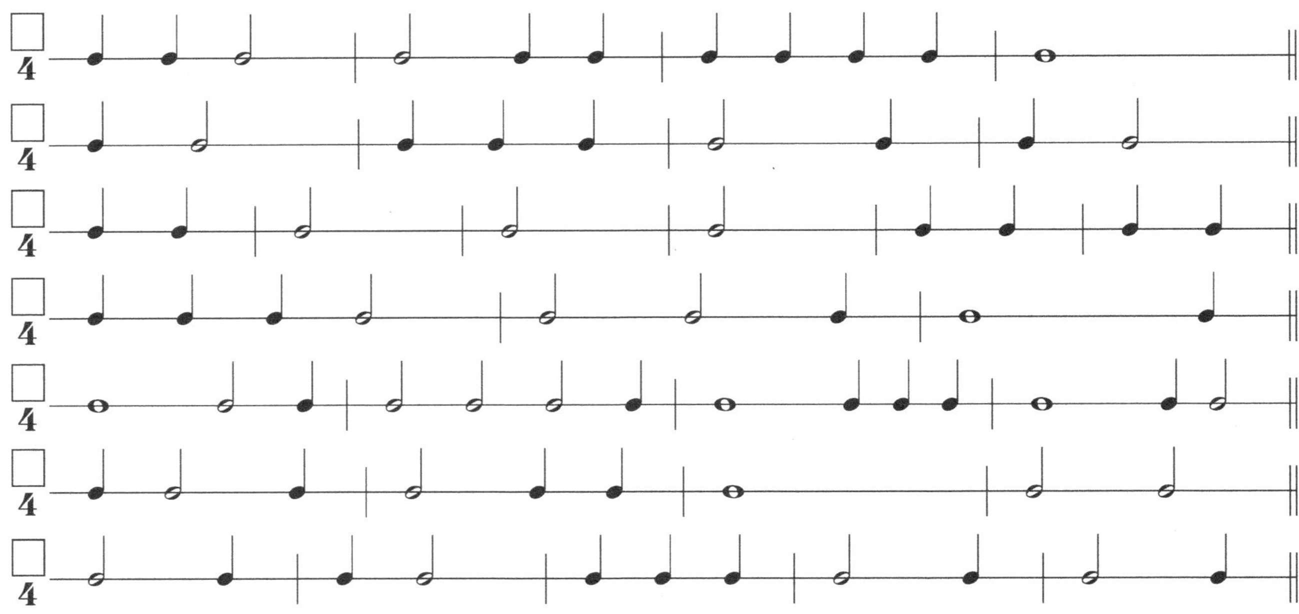

YOU'VE GOT RHYTHM!

Using the following notes and rests, create two different four measure rhythm patterns. Share your rhythm pattern with a partner. Check each other's work. Clap and count the pattern your partner created.

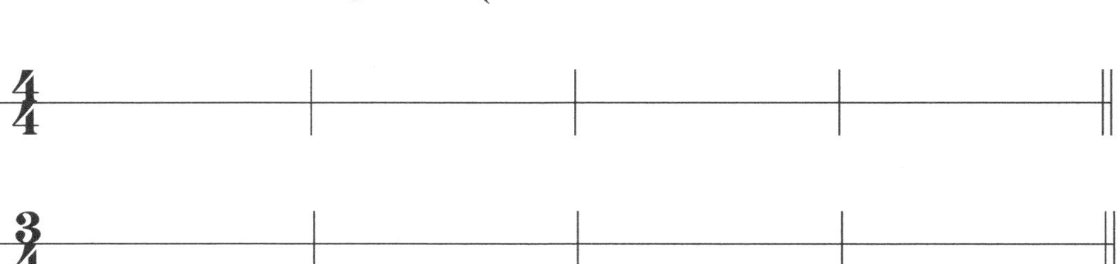

PROJECT: RHYTHM MANIA

Dividing rhythm patterns into measures makes them easier to read. How many different ways could you divide these quarter notes? Circle the time signatures that you could use.

The next pattern uses quarter and half notes. How many ways could they be divided? Circle the time signatures you could use.

READING RHYTHM

Name _______________________________

Musicians count rhythms in various ways. One common way to count rhythm uses numbers.

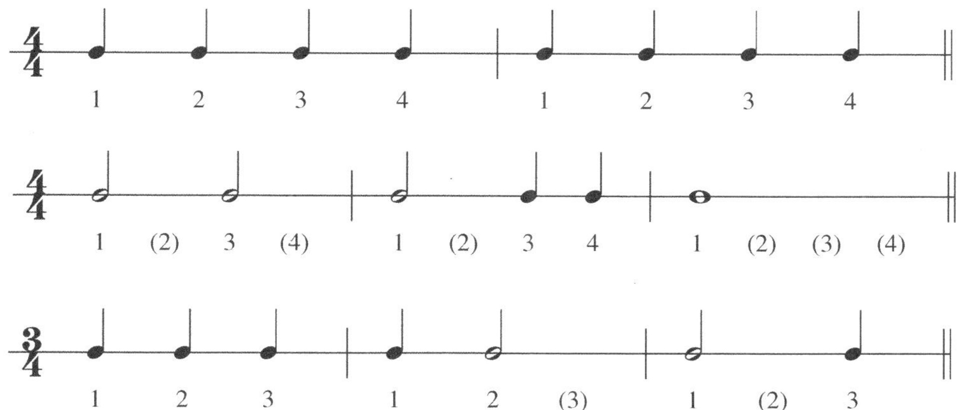

When clapping and counting a rhythm with rests, whisper the count but do not clap. Remember, rests are the symbol for silence.

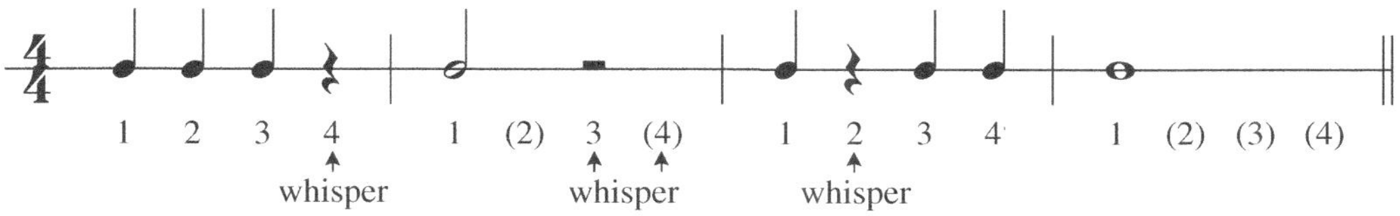

RHYTHM WORD SEARCH

Find the following hidden rhythm words.

bar line
beat
measure
notate
note
quarter
rest
rhythm
time signature
whole
meter

Y	O	J	H	K	U	O	W	D	V	Y	W	K	E	L
R	E	B	A	R	L	I	N	E	M	U	H	T	Z	J
M	R	W	S	X	T	N	S	Q	T	S	O	E	K	A
P	E	R	U	S	V	R	I	B	U	E	L	R	B	W
W	P	T	E	G	U	B	N	E	T	A	E	H	V	M
X	P	R	E	H	F	N	N	A	M	N	R	Y	I	X
O	A	M	S	R	L	X	T	T	W	O	J	T	M	B
L	Z	R	U	M	X	O	F	Z	Z	T	V	H	E	U
G	V	Y	S	W	N	N	N	F	O	E	B	M	G	R
I	Z	Q	M	E	A	S	U	R	E	V	N	Y	V	C
L	T	I	M	E	S	I	G	N	A	T	U	R	E	G
G	A	H	G	E	V	Q	R	S	X	E	H	Z	V	S

RHYTHMS TO READ

Write in the counting below the notes as shown and then clap and count aloud each of the following rhythms. Check the time signature before you clap and count each example.

Note and Rest Value Review

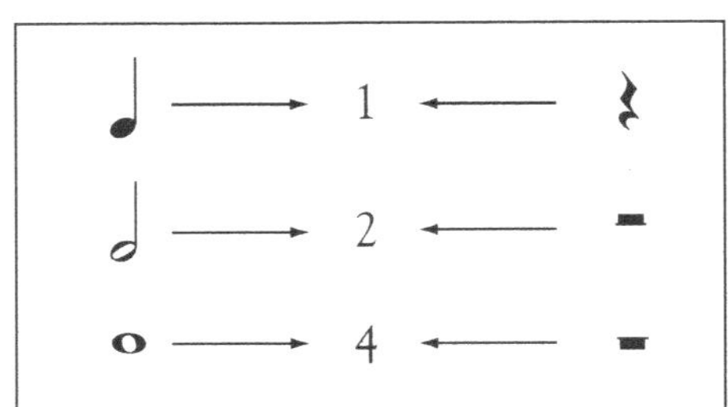

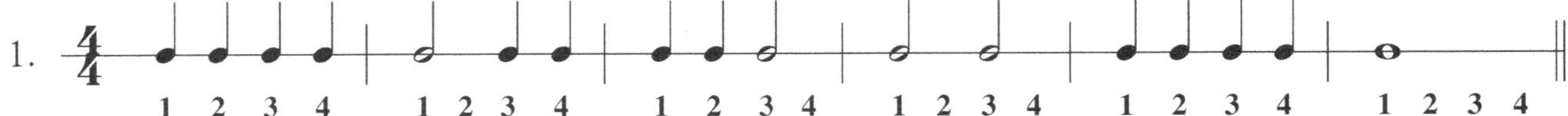

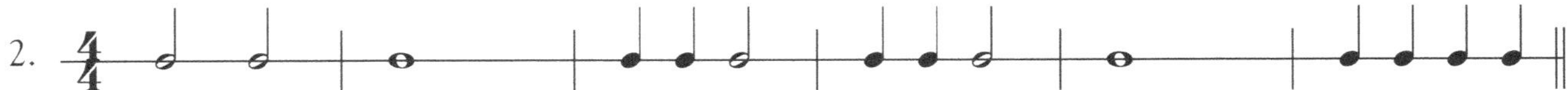

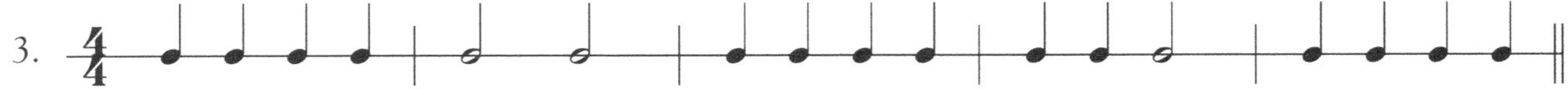

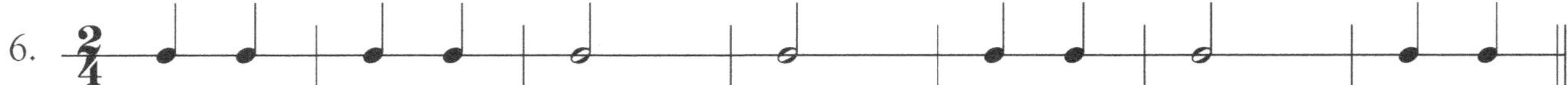

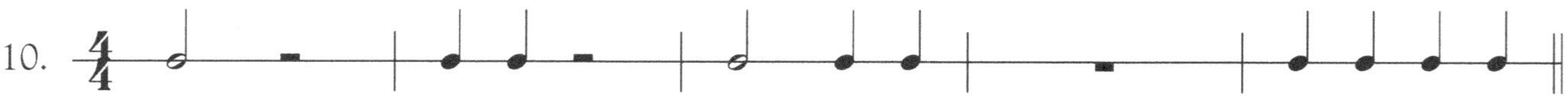

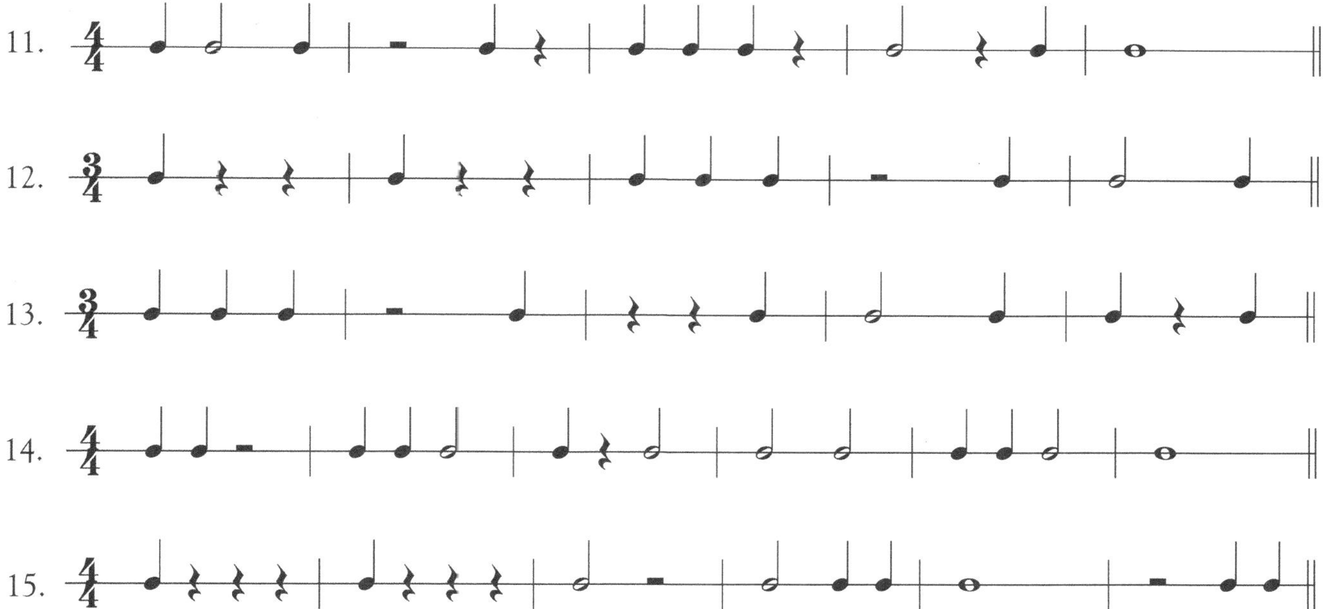

CONDUCTING

A conductor musically communicates the beat and time signature through the use of conducting patterns. Using your hand or a pencil in place of the conductor's baton, practice conducting the following patterns. Count the beats as you conduct.

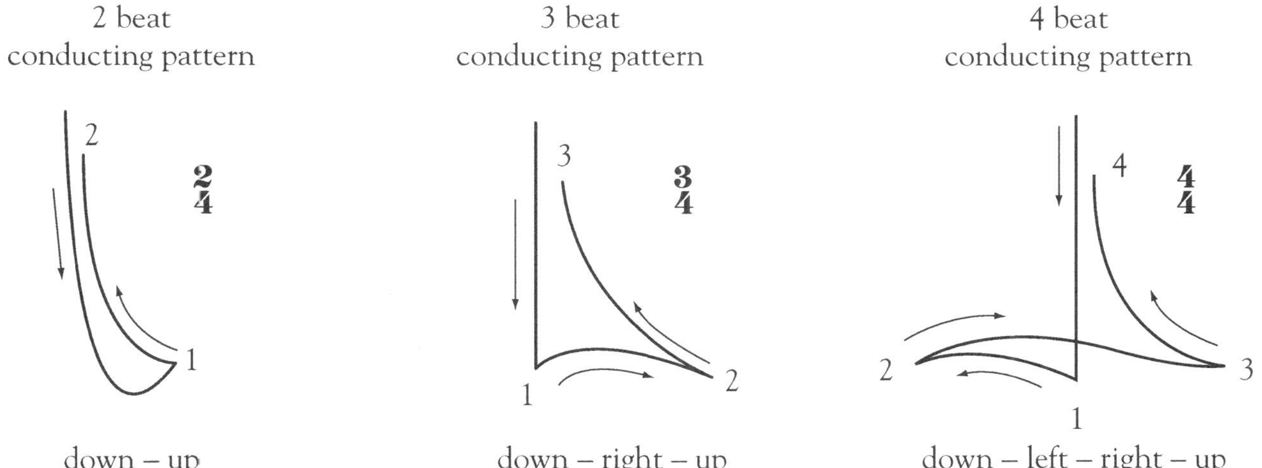

CONDUCTING RHYTHM

Practice Rhythms to Read on the previous page again, this time conducting as you count.

PROJECT: YOU'RE THE MAESTRO!

Hum or sing each of the following songs as you conduct. Which conducting pattern will you use for each song? Fill in the time signature when you have decided.

______My Country 'Tis of Thee

______Jingle Bells

______Frosty the Snowman

______Mary Had a Little Lamb

______Yankee Doodle

______Go Tell Aunt Rhody

EIGHTH AND SIXTEENTH NOTES AND RESTS

Name ____

The beat in music can be divided into smaller values. These values, or notes, receive fractions, or parts of the steady beat.

EIGHTH NOTES

♪ = 1/2 beat

𝄾 = 1/2 beat

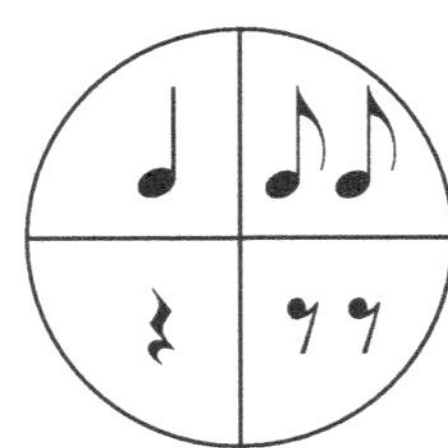

Eighth notes can be beamed together to make them easier to read.

♪ ♪ = ♫   ♪ ♪ ♪ ♪ = ♫♫

Draw four more eighth notes with flags.

Draw four more pairs of beamed eighth notes.

Draw four more eighth rests.

SIXTEENTH NOTES

♬ = 1/4 beat

𝄿 = 1/4 beat

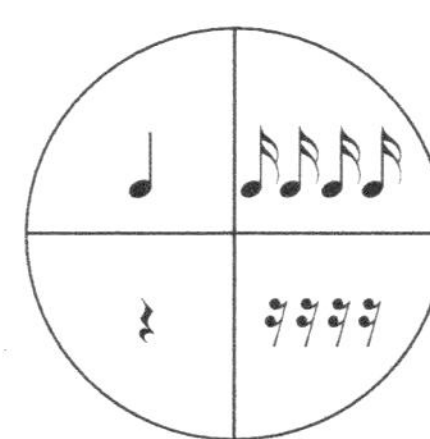

Sixteenth notes can be beamed together to make them easier to read.

Draw four more sixteenth notes with flags.

Draw four more groups of sixteenth notes beamed together.

MUSIC MATH: TRUE OR FALSE?

1. T F   ♫ = ♩
2. T F ♬ = ♩
3. T F ♫ + ♩ = ♩
4. T F ♬ + ♫ = ♩
5. T F 𝄾 + ♪ + ♩ = 𝅝

6. T F ♬ = ♫
7. T F 𝄾 + 𝄾 = ♩
8. T F 𝄽 + 𝄾 + 𝄾 = ♩
9. T F ♬ + ♩ = 𝅝
10. T F ♪ + ♪ + 𝄾 + ♩ = 𝅝

COUNTING EIGHTHS AND SIXTEENTHS

Here is a way to clap and count eighth and sixteenth notes. Clap and count each note.

Clap and count this rhythm. Describe what happens to the note values in each measure.

COUNT OFF!

Clap and count the following rhythm patterns. Remember to divide the beat when you count the eighth and sixteenth notes.

RHYTHM WIZARDRY

Create your own four measure rhythm patterns.
Use each of the following note values at least once:

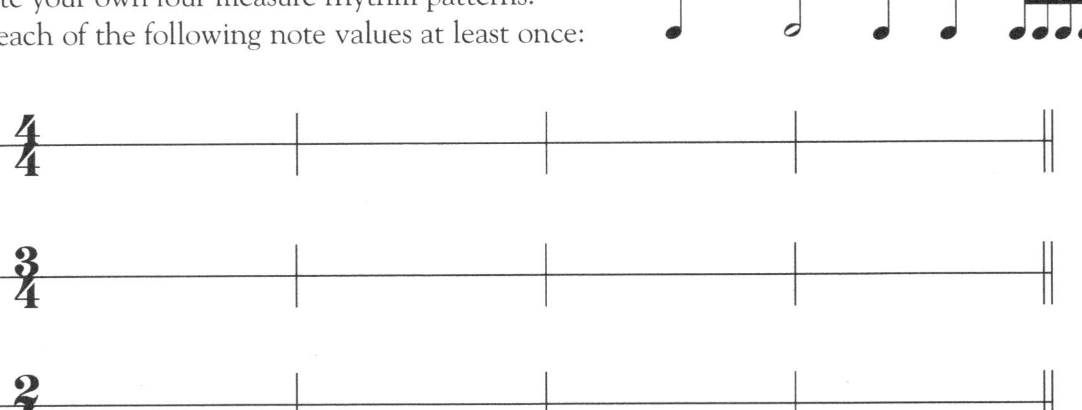

TIME FOR A REST REVIEW

Match the following rests to their correct name.

eighth rest

sixteenth rest

quarter rest

half rest

whole rest

PROJECT: NAME GAME

Create a rhythm that represents the name of each of the famous Americans below,
as in the example.

John F. Kennedy

George Washington

Rosa Parks

Alexander Hamilton

Eleanor Roosevelt

Ben Franklin

Martin Luther King

Susan B. Anthony

Harriet Tubman

John Glenn

Your Name:_______________________________________

TIES AND DOTTED NOTES

Name ______________________________

A **tie** is a curved line used to increase the value of a note. The value of a tied note equals the total of both notes added ("tied") together.

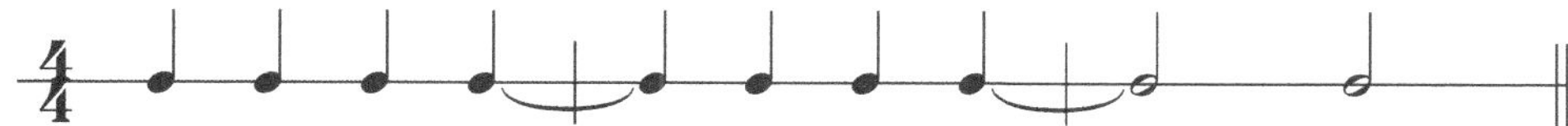

Ties can increase the value of a note across the bar line.

Clap the following rhythms containing tied notes. Do not clap on the second note of the tied notes; keep holding on to the first note for the full value of both notes tied together.

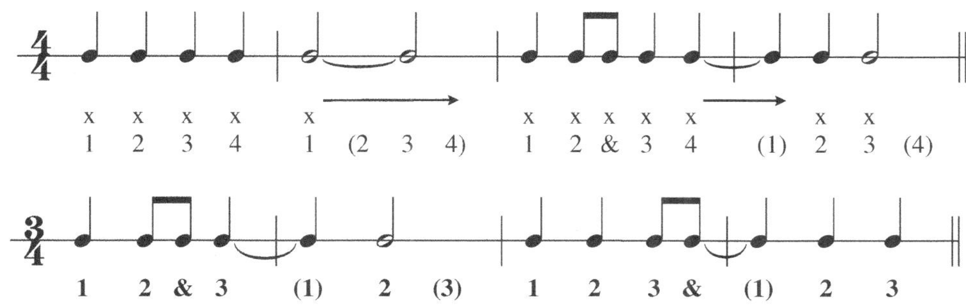

Another way to lengthen a note is to add a **dot**. A dot increases the value (duration) by half of the original value of the note it follows.

ADD A DOT

Complete the note value chart to the right:

𝅘𝅥 = 1 beat	𝅘𝅥. =
𝅗𝅥 = 2 beats	𝅗𝅥. =
𝅝 = 4 beats	𝅝. =
𝅘𝅥𝅮 = ½ beat	𝅘𝅥𝅮. =
𝄽 = 1 beat	𝄽. =

TIME TO DIVIDE

Draw bar lines to divide the following rhythm patterns into measures.

PROJECT: FIND THE MISSING DOTS!

Each measure below contains a note that is missing a dot. Add the dot to the correct note to complete each measure. When you are finished, compare your answers with a partner and take turns clapping the rhythms.

CHALLENGE

For each set of tied notes below, notate one dotted note that equals the same value.

1. =

2. =

3. =

4. =

MORE ABOUT TIME SIGNATURES

Name ____

Early in your music study, you may have noticed that **time signatures** almost always had the number four as the bottom number, giving the quarter note one beat. Other note values are also used as the basic unit of beat. This is indicated by a number other than four as the bottom number of a time signature.

When the basic unit of beat changes, so do the values of the other notes.

WHO'S GOT THE BEAT?

Write in the counting for the rhythms below. Be sure to note the time signature to decide which note will get one beat. After you write in the counting, clap and count the rhythms.

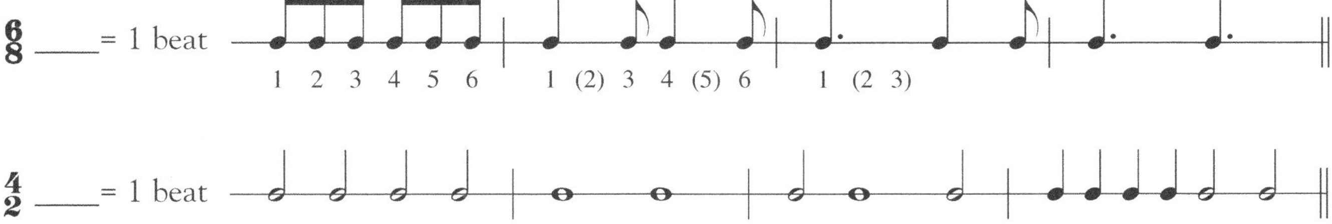

RHYTHM RELATIVITY

Divide each example into measures according to the time signature given. Clap and count the rhythms to check your work.

RHYTHM CROSSWORD

Across

3. The symbol for silence in music

4. A person who uses a baton to show the musical beat

7. The space between two bar lines

8. A short line pointing up or down on a note head

Down

1. This divides notes into measures

2. When added to a note, this adds half to the note's value

5. A curved line connecting two notes

6. A regular, recurring sound in music

PROJECT: WHERE'S THE BEAT?

Complete a rhythm pattern for each of the time signatures below. Use as many different note and rest values as you can. Share your examples with a partner, taking turns clapping the rhythms you've both created.

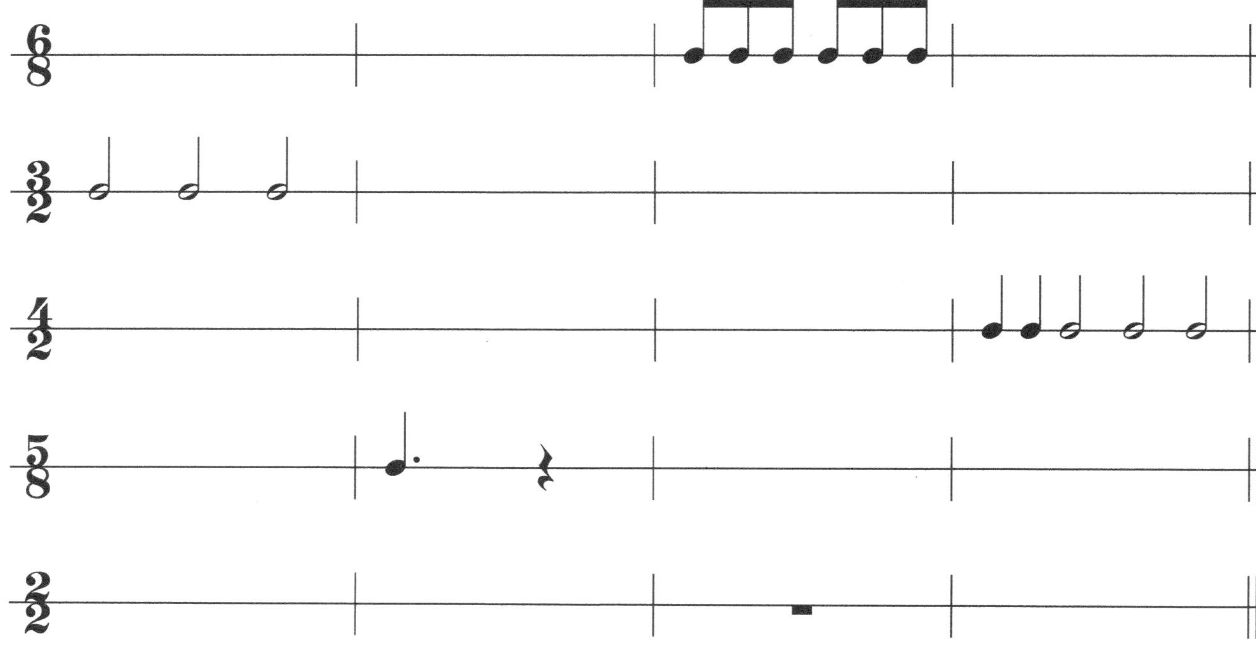

SYNCOPATION

Name _______________________

In many rhythm patterns, the strongest beat occurs on the first beat of the measure.

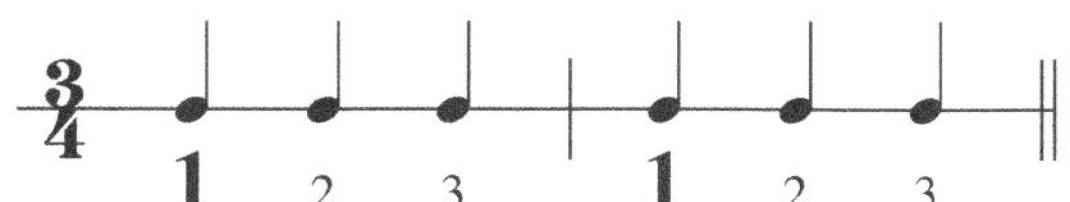 

In **4/4** time, the strongest beat falls on beat one as well, with a secondary beat on beat three.

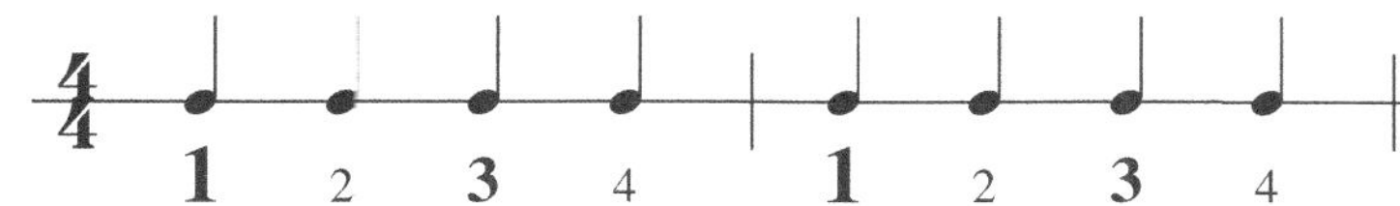

In **6/8** time, strong beats occur on beat one and beat four.

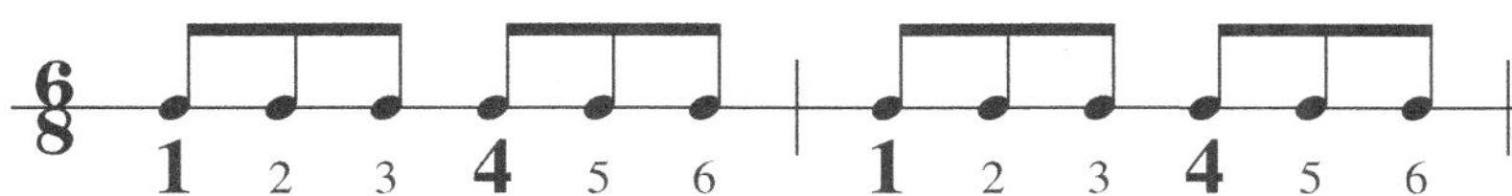

When beats other than these receive a strong accent, we hear **syncopation**. Syncopation in music is when an accent occurs on what is usually a weak beat in a measure. One of the most common syncopated rhythms is when the eighth note appears on beat one, followed by a quarter note.

DISCOVERING SYNCOPATION

Clap the steady eighth note rhythm.

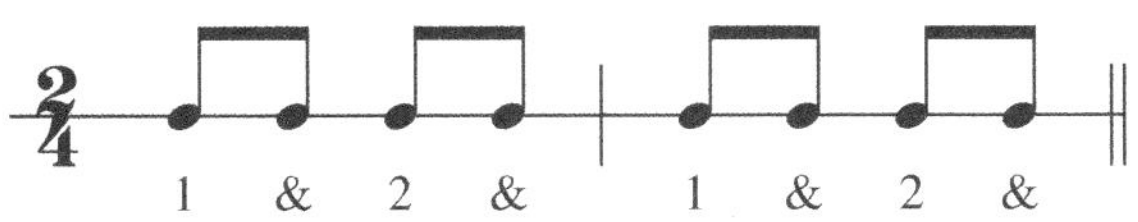

Clap the eighth note rhythm with a tie added.

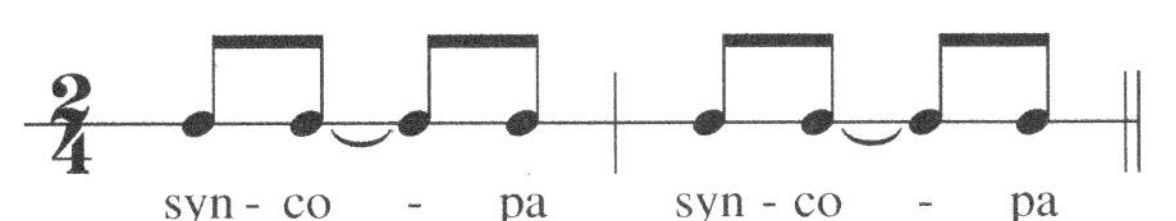 or 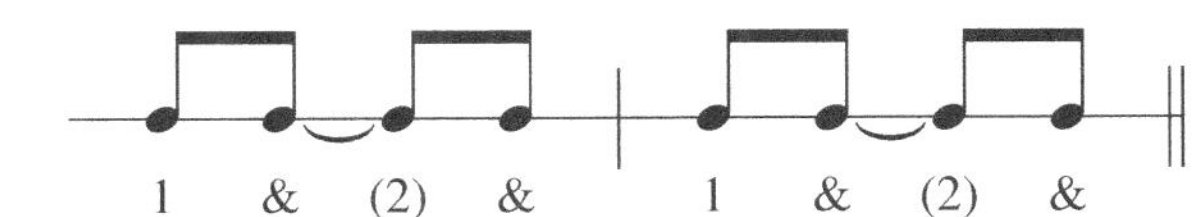

Clap this same rhythm written a different way.

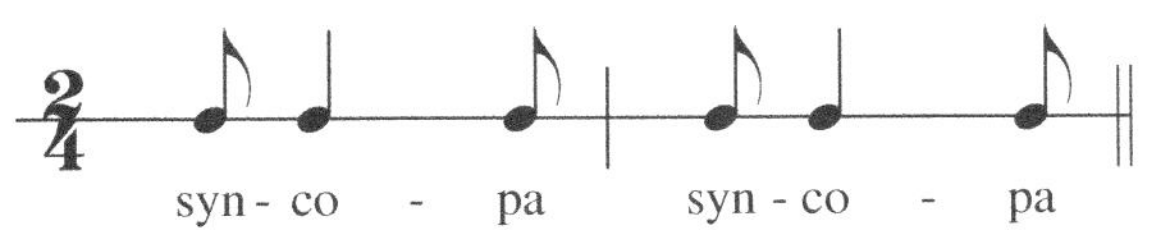 or 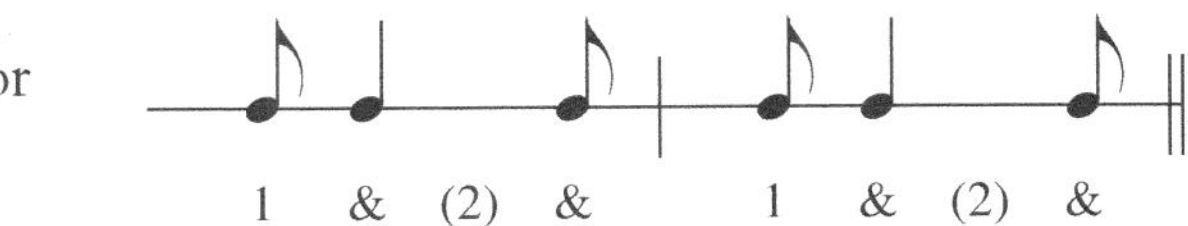

CREATING SYNCOPATION

Clap the following rhythms in two ways. First, clap the rhythms letting the accents fall where they usually do.

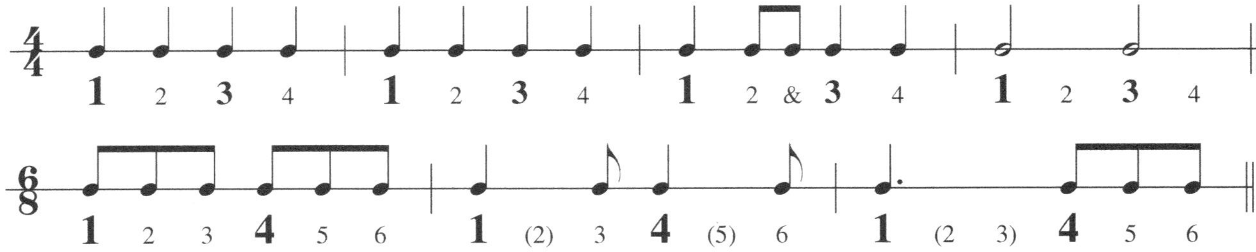

Now accent the beats differently, as indicated by the accent marks below. > is the musical sign for **accent**, or extra emphasis.

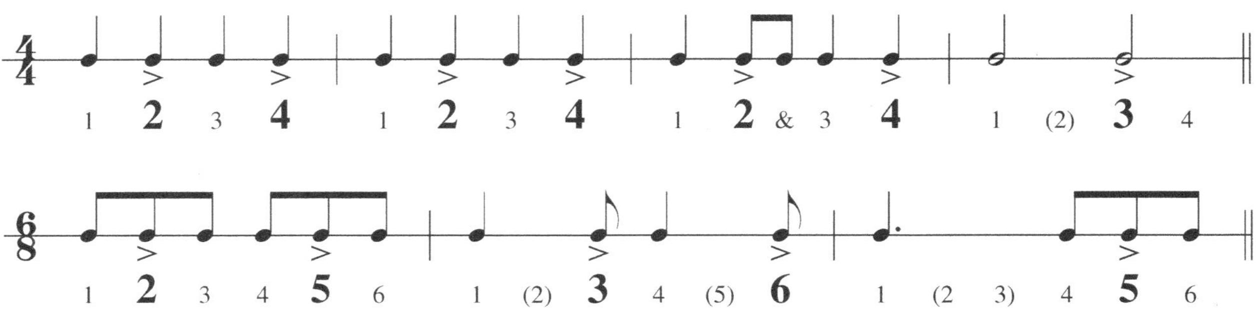

Can you feel the syncopation? Was it easy to accent the beats the second time? Explain your answer.

____

____

____

____

SYNCOPATION CHALLENGE

1. Add bar lines to the following rhythms. Use a double bar line at the end of each line.
2. Write in the counting underneath the notes.
3. Clap and count the rhythms.

PROJECT: SYNCOPATION AGGRAVATION

Each of the short rhythm examples contains at least one measure of syncopation.

    1. Write in the counting under the notes in each measure.

    2. Clap and say the words for each example.

    3. Circle all measures containing syncopated rhythms.

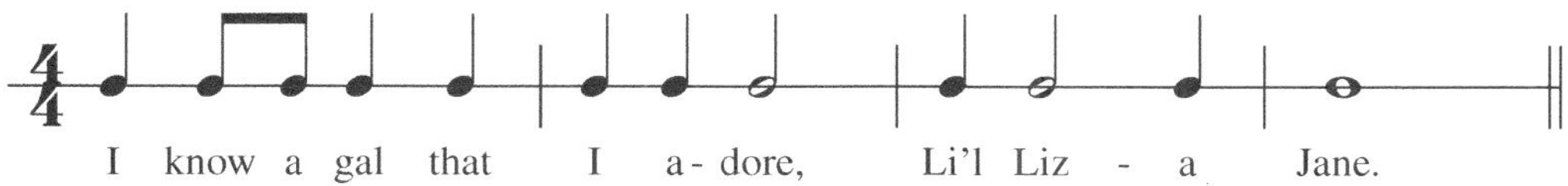

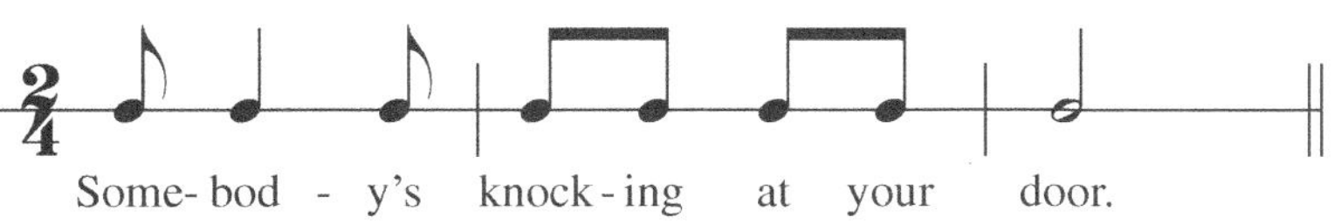

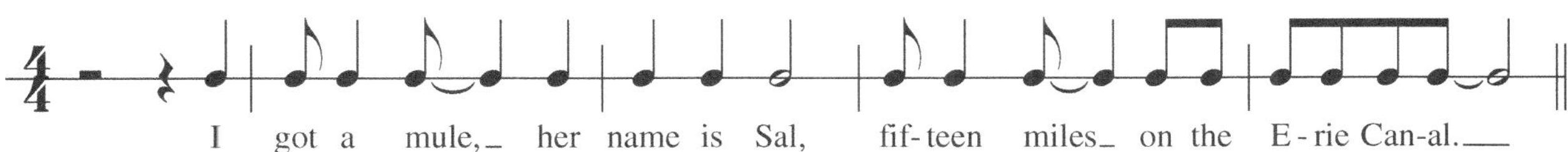

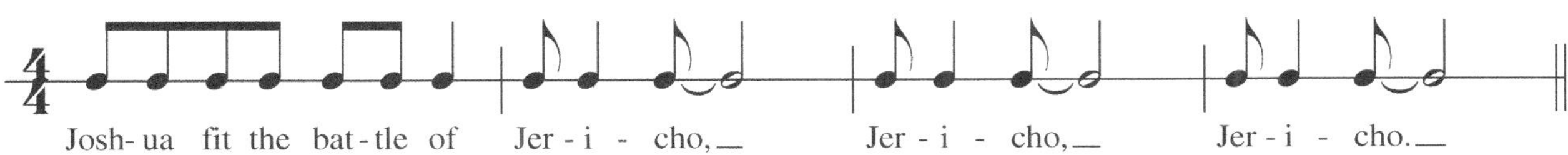

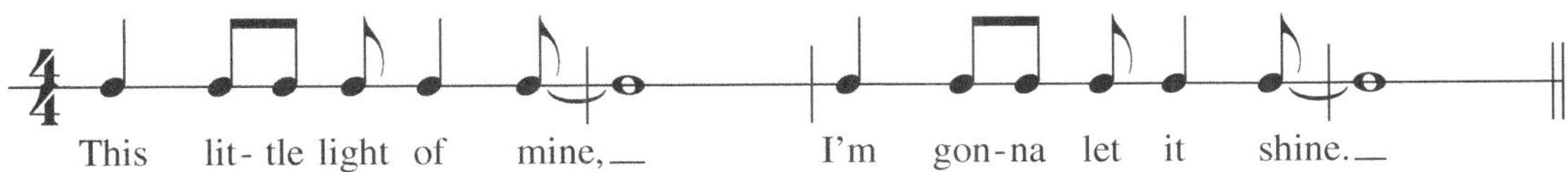

ELEMENTS OF RHYTHM QUIZ

Name ____

A. Mark the following True or False.

T F 1. Beat is a regular, recurring sound in music.

T F 2. Beat can be slow or fast.

T F 3. Rests are symbols for sound in music.

T F 4. A double bar is placed at the beginning of a measure.

T F 5. The top number of a time signature indicates which note gets one beat.

T F 6. Eighth notes can be written with a flag or beamed.

T F 7. Time signatures always have a 4 as the bottom number.

T F 8. A dot next to a note lengthens the note by 2 beats.

T F 9. Sixteenth notes should always be beamed.

T F 10. ♪♪♪ is an example of syncopation.

T F 11. ♩ = ♫♩

T F 12. 𝄽 = ♪

B. Arrange the following note values from shortest to longest.

____

C. Using notes or rests, complete the following equations.

In $\frac{4}{4}$ time:

1. ♩ + _______ = 4 beats

2. ♫♩ + _______ = 4 beats

3. ♩. + ♪ + _______ = 4 beats

4. 𝅝 − _______ = 2 beats

5. ♩. − _______ = 1 beat

6. ♩. + _______ = 3 beats

In $\frac{6}{8}$ time:

7. ♩. + _______ = 6 beats

8. ♩ + _______ = 6 beats

9. ♫♩ + _______ = 6 beats

10. ♩ + _______ = 3 beats

11. ♩ − _______ = 2 beats

12. ♪ + ♩ + _______ = 6 beats

D. Each example below contains one incorrect measure. Show what changes are needed to make these measures correct. The first one has been done for you.

E. Fill in the missing time signatures in each example below.

MELODIC NOTATION

Name _______________________________

Music is written on a graph of five lines and four spaces called a **staff**. The lines and spaces are numbered from bottom to top.

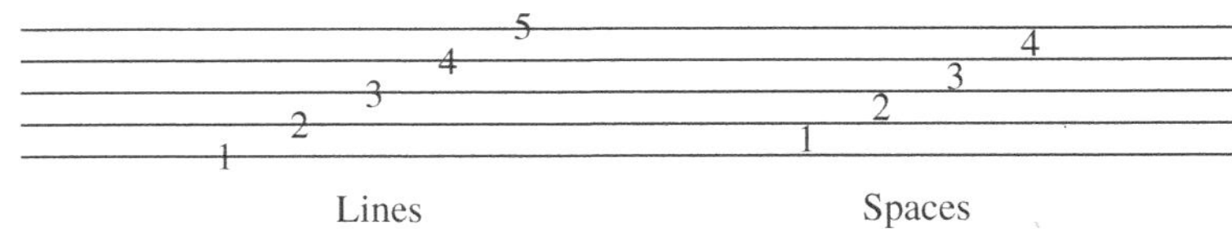

Pitch (musical sound) is represented when notes are placed on the staff. A note can be placed *on* a line or *in* a space. The higher the pitch, the higher it is placed on the staff.

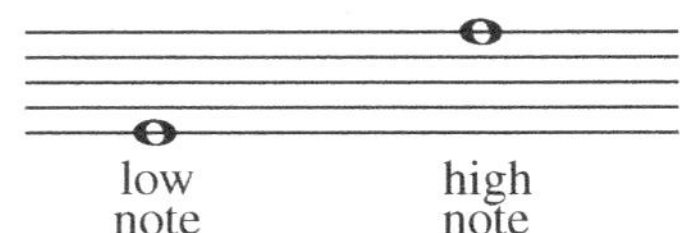

LINE OR SPACE?

Draw notes on the staff below.

line note	space note	line note	line note	space note	space note	line note

high note	low note	2nd space note	1st line note	4th space note	2nd line note	5th line note

A **clef** is a symbol placed at the beginning of a staff. The most common clefs are **treble** and **bass**. Notes written on the treble clef sound higher than notes written on the bass clef. Instruments that use treble clef notes include flute, clarinet, violin and trumpet. Instruments that play in bass clef include trombone, cello and tuba.

Practice tracing the treble and bass clefs below and then draw two more of each on the staff. Carefully note exactly where each part of the clef is placed on the staff.

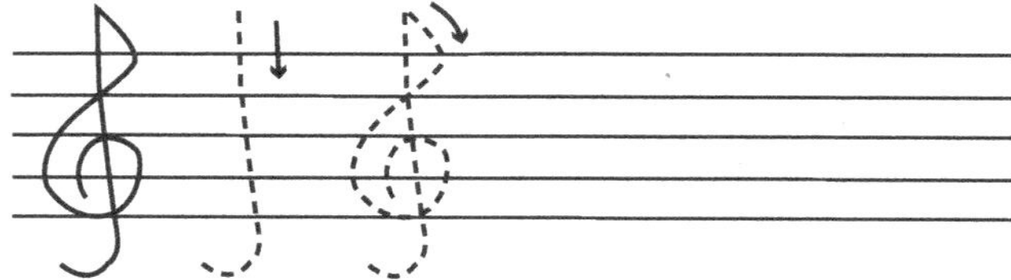

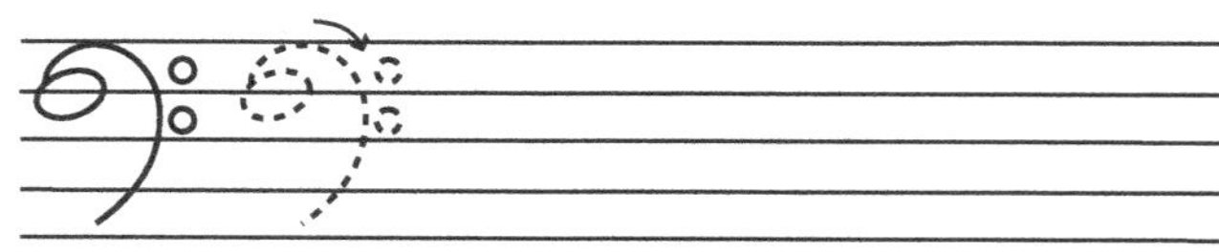

A **grand staff** is a grouping of two **staves** (plural of staff) connected by a brace and a bracket. Piano, organ and harp use the grand staff. Often music for several voices or instruments playing together will be notated on a grand staff.

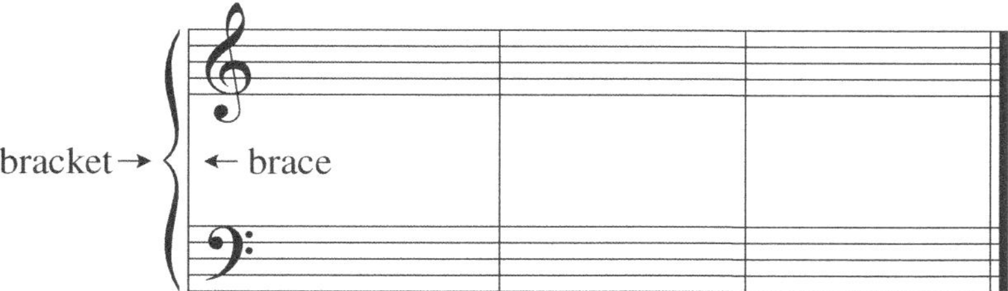

PROJECT: UNDER CONSTRUCTION

Construct a grand staff in the space below. You may wish to use a straight edge or ruler to draw the staff lines neatly. Include the following elements:

treble staff and clef

bass staff and clef

bracket

brace

whole note on treble staff line 1

whole note on treble staff space 3

whole note on bass staff line 4

whole note on bass staff space 1

READING TREBLE CLEF

Name ____

The **treble clef** is used for notes of higher pitch. The treble clef is also called the G clef because the curl of the treble clef circles the G line on the treble staff.

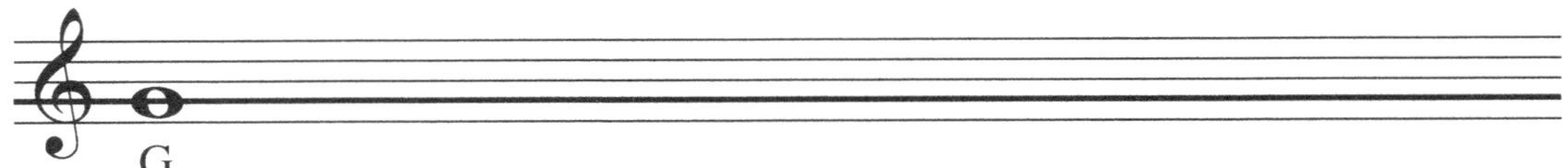

In the **musical alphabet** there are 7 letter names for pitches: **A B C D E F G**. These letter names repeat as the pitches move higher and lower.

Write the letters of the musical alphabet starting with **A**_______________________

Write the letters of the musical alphabet backwards. _______________________

One way to identify pitches on the treble staff is to think of the line and space notes separately. The pitches in the spaces of the treble staff spell the word **FACE**. To remember the names of the lines of the treble staff, just think of the phrase Every Good Boy Does Fine.

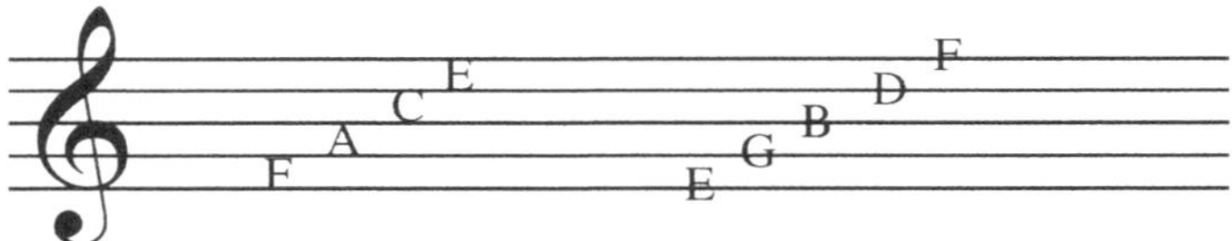

TEST YOURSELF!

Name the following pitches on the treble staff.

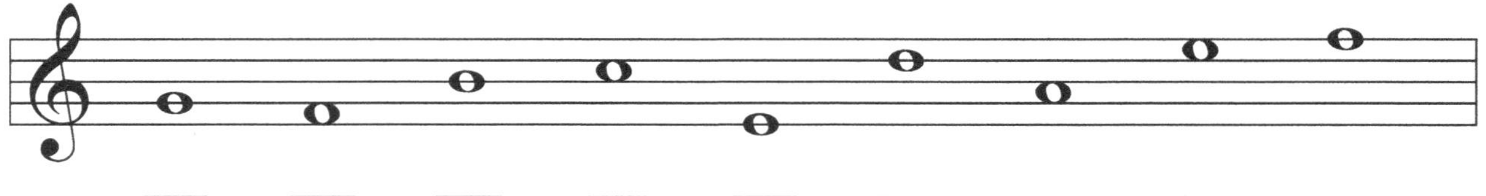

Notate the pitches given under the treble staff below.

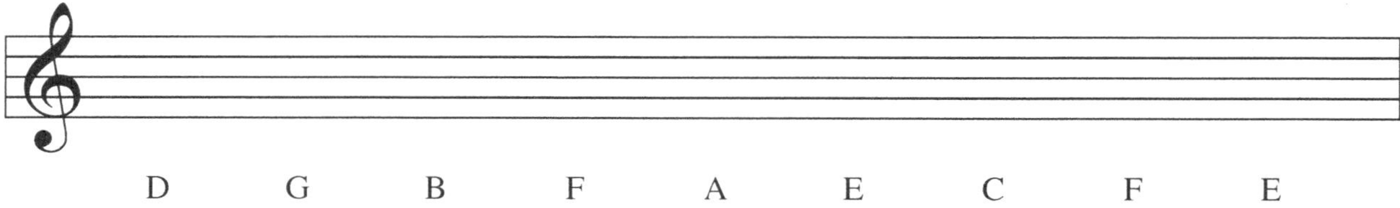

MUSICAL WORDS

The following measures below contain pitches that will spell a word. Name the notes to discover the word.

The treble clef notes correspond with the keys in the upper half of the piano. The higher the note on the staff, the higher that note will be on the keyboard.

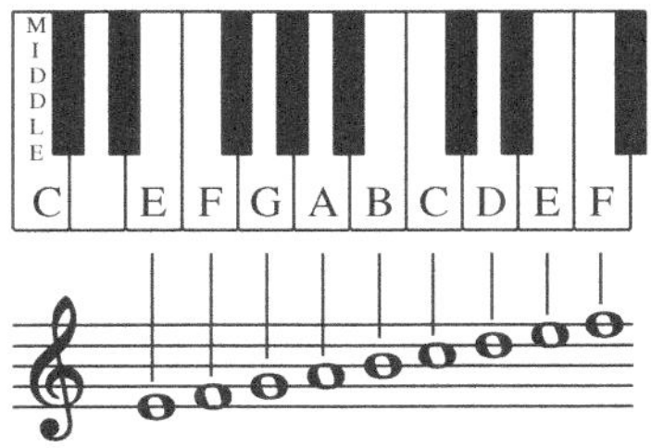

KEYBOARD MATCH

Draw a line connecting each note on the staff to the keyboard. The first one has been done for you.

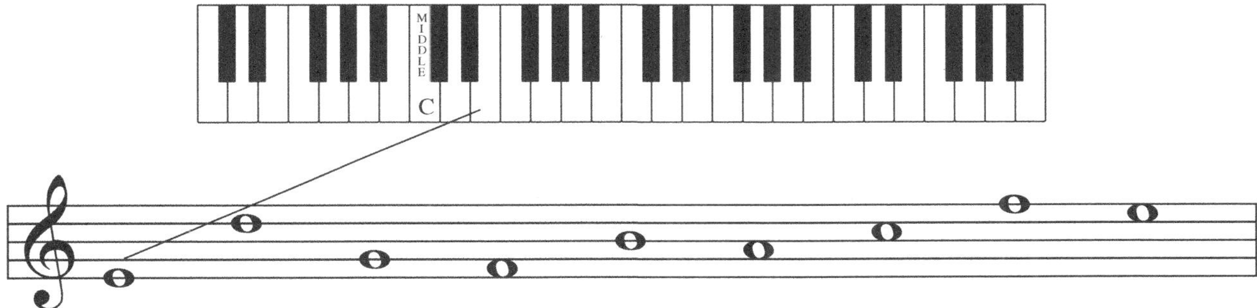

PROJECT: TELL A STORY

Write a short story using 10 words that can be spelled using notes in the treble staff. Remember the musical alphabet is: A B C D E F G. First write your words on the staff below, and then write your story, underlining or highlighting the words you spelled on the staff.

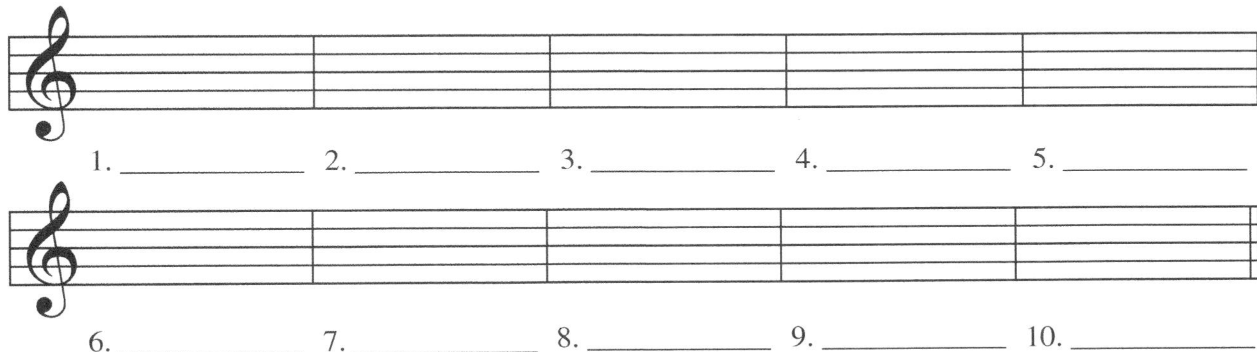

READING BASS CLEF

Name ____

The **bass clef** (bass is pronounced "base") is used for notes of lower pitch. It is also called the F clef, because the two dots of the clef surround the F line of the bass staff.

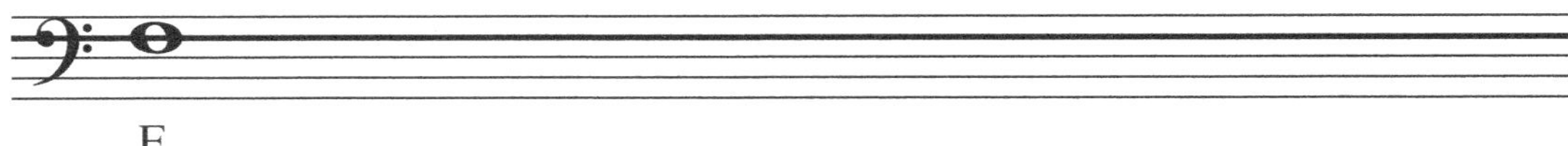

The pitch names for the spaces in this clef are **ACEG**. The line notes in bass clef are **GBDFA**. Here is one way to remember the line and space notes on the bass blef.

spaces: **A**ll **C**ows **E**at **G**rass   lines: **G**ood **B**irds **D**on't **F**ly **A**lone

Write at least one other way to remember the line and space notes.

spaces: A_________   C_________   E_________   G_________

lines: G_________   B_________   D_________   F_________   A_________

KNOW THE BASS NOTES

Identify the following bass clef notes.

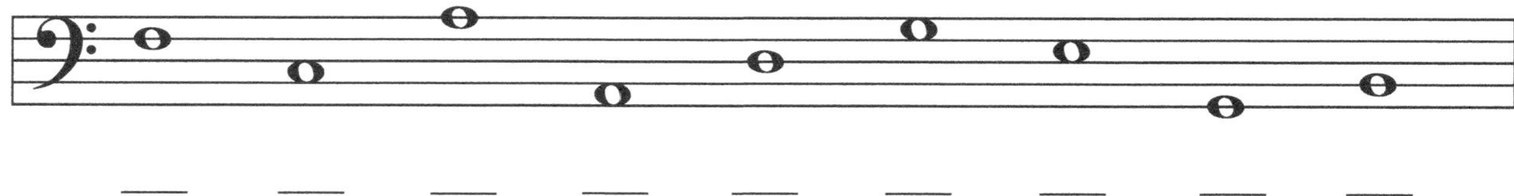

___   ___   ___   ___   ___   ___   ___   ___   ___   ___

Notate the pitches given under the bass staff below.

F   C   D   A   G   E   B   G   A

The pitches written on the bass staff fall below middle C on the piano keyboard.

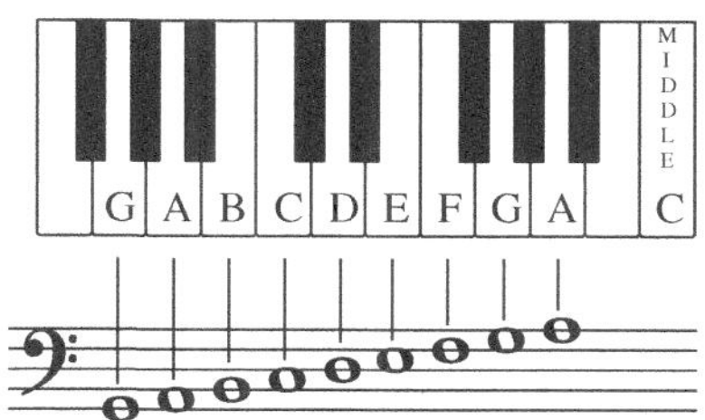

KEYBOARD MATCH

Draw a line connecting each note on the staff to the piano keyboard. Remember, all notes in the bass clef are below middle C!

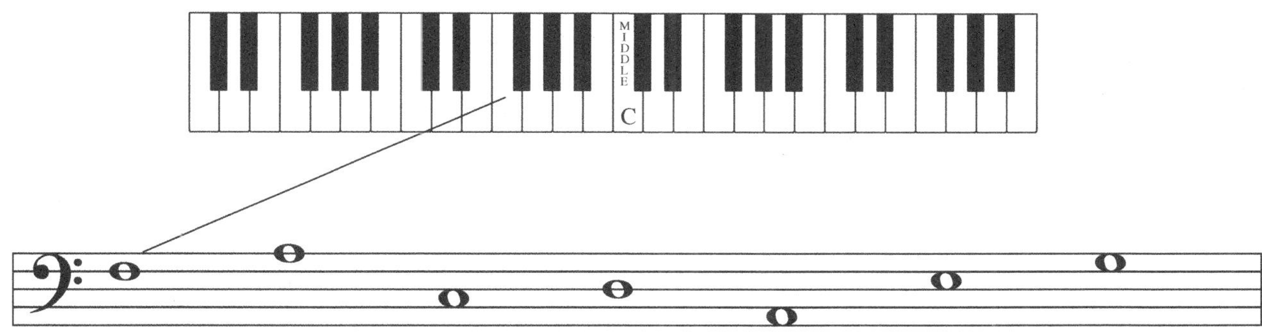

SPELLING THE BASS CLEF

Each measure below contains notes that will spell a word. Identify the pitches to discover the word.

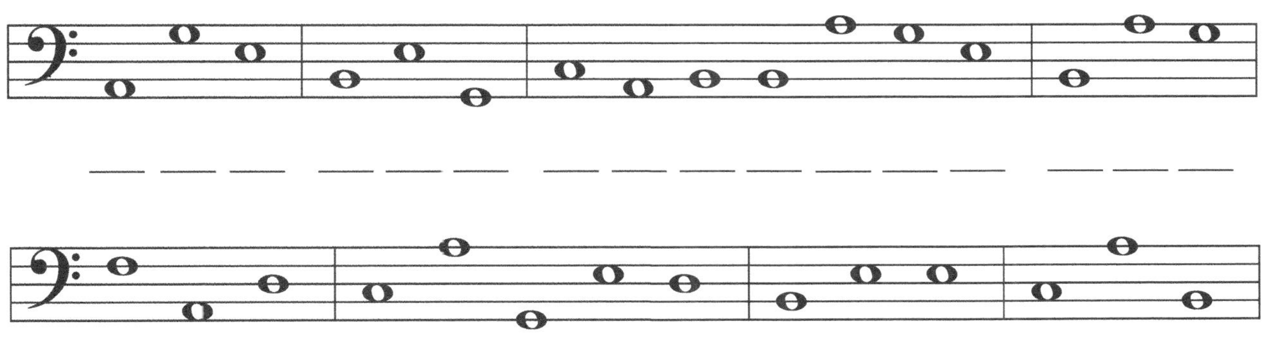

PROJECT: CLEF SLEUTH

For each word spelled using the music alphabet, it is written in treble clef and in bass clef. One of the spellings is wrong. Write in the pitch names. Then circle the correct spelling of the word.

add

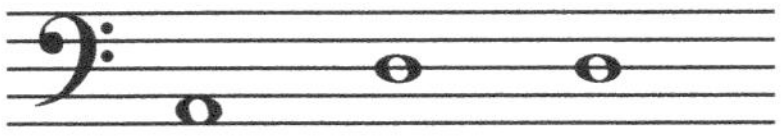

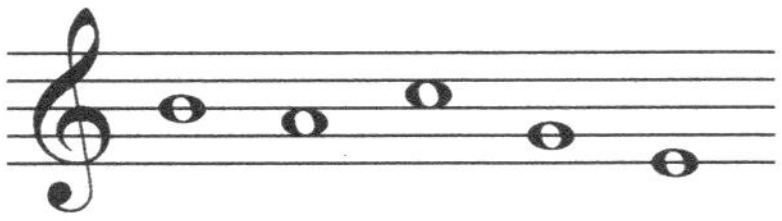

badge

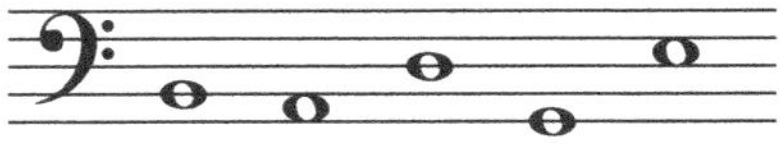

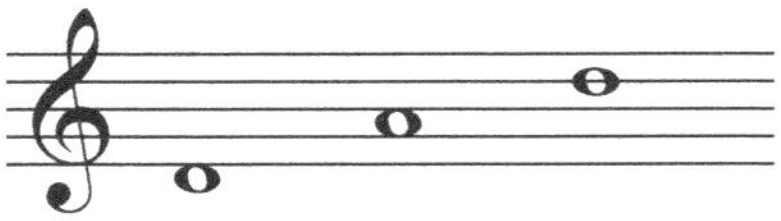

dad

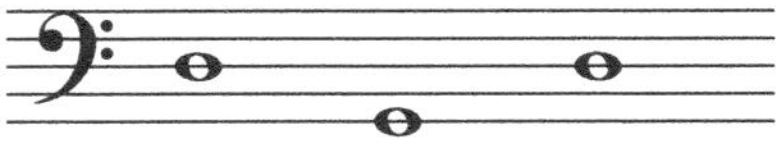

bed

beef

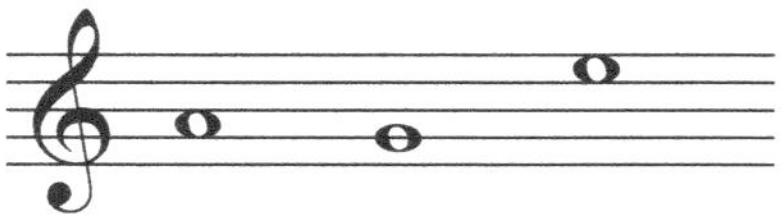

age

baggage

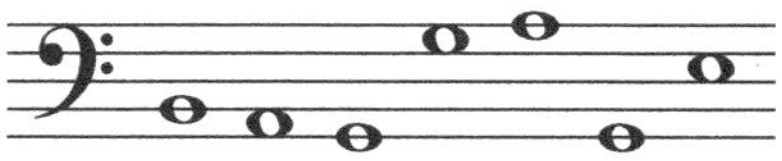

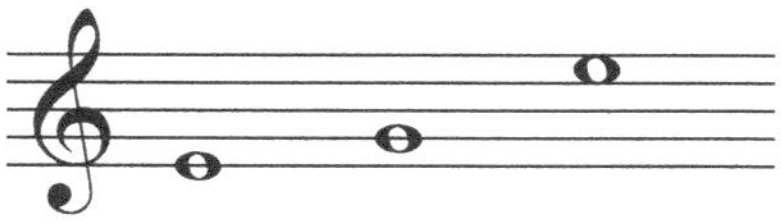

egg

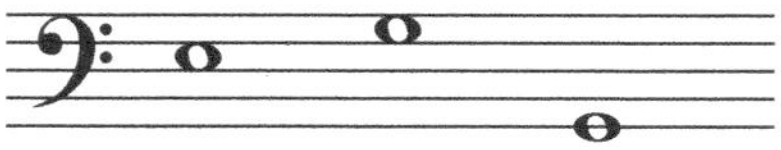

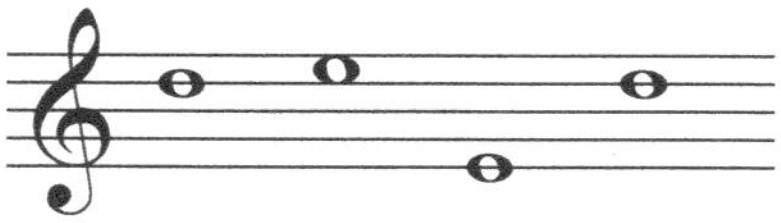

deed

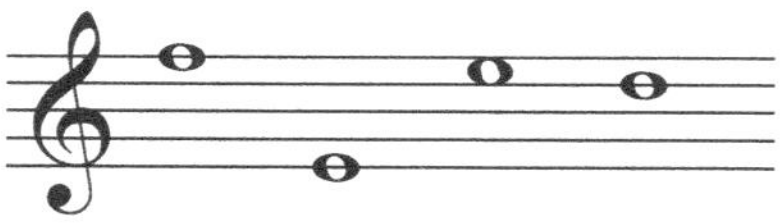

feed

READING LEDGER LINES AND MOVEABLE CLEFS

Name _______________________________

Notes that extend above or below the staff use **ledger lines**. These additional ledger lines extend the staff to notate very high or very low pitches.

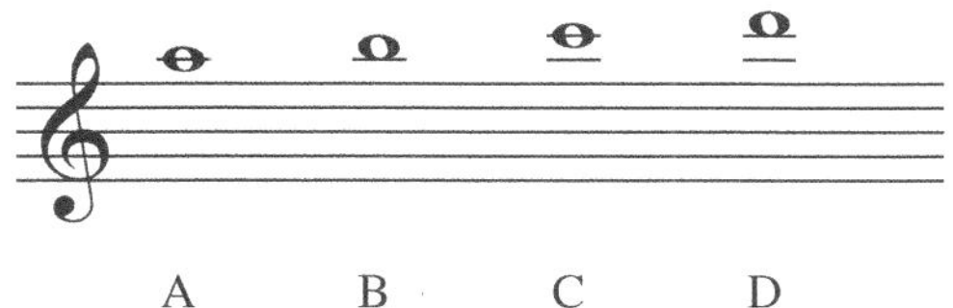

LEDGER LINE PRACTICE

Name the following notes written on ledger lines.

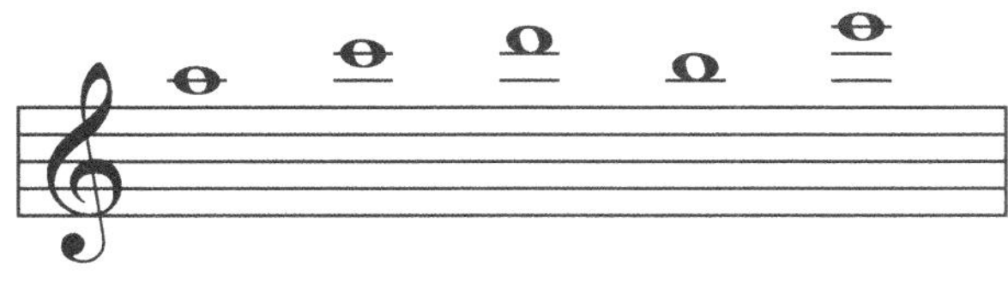

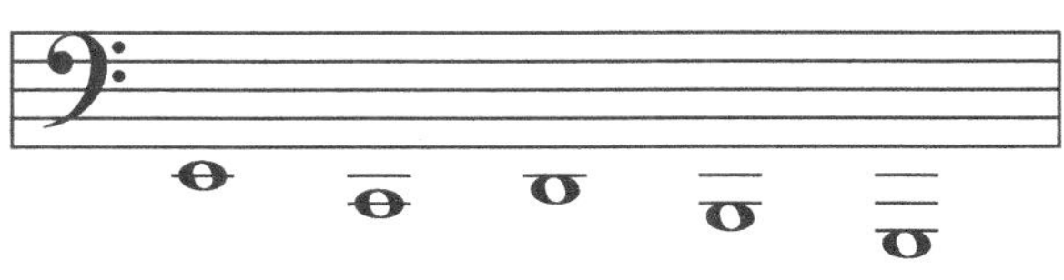

MIDDLE C

The most easily recognized ledger line is middle C. Did you know that middle C designates the middle of the grand staff, and not the middle of the piano keyboard? The notes in the middle of the grand staff can be written on either staff by using ledger lines.

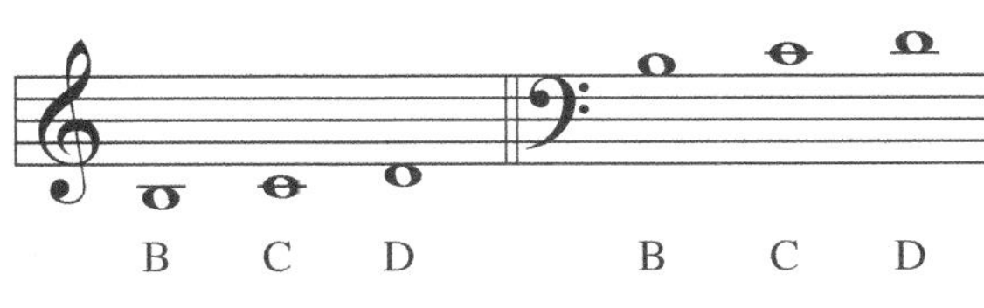

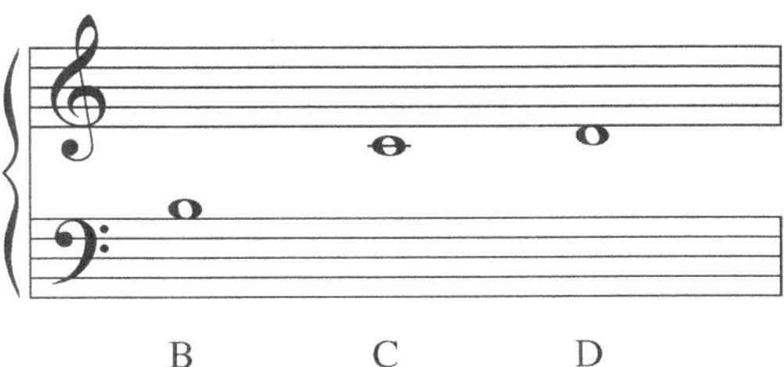

ANOTHER WAY TO WRITE IT!

For each of the given notes, notate the same pitch in the opposite clef using ledger lines.

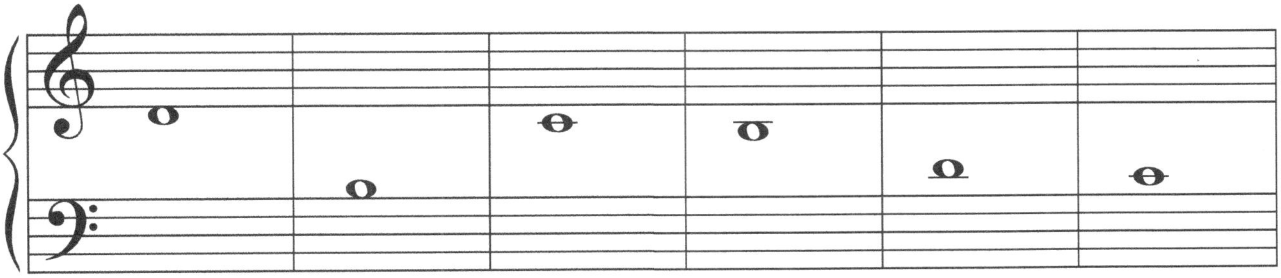

MORE CLEFS

Although treble and bass are the most common clef signs used in music, there are other clefs used regularly. Remember, a clef is a symbol that designates where a particular note will be placed on the staff. In early music, **movable clefs** could be placed on any line. Today two of these moveable clefs remain in use. The **alto clef** designates the middle line as middle C and is used primarily for viola. The **tenor clef** designates the 4th line as middle C and is sometimes used for cello, bassoon and trombone.

MOVEABLE CLEF CHALLENGE

Spell the following words using moveable clefs. Before you spell each word, check to see which clef is used and which note the clef identifies on the staff.

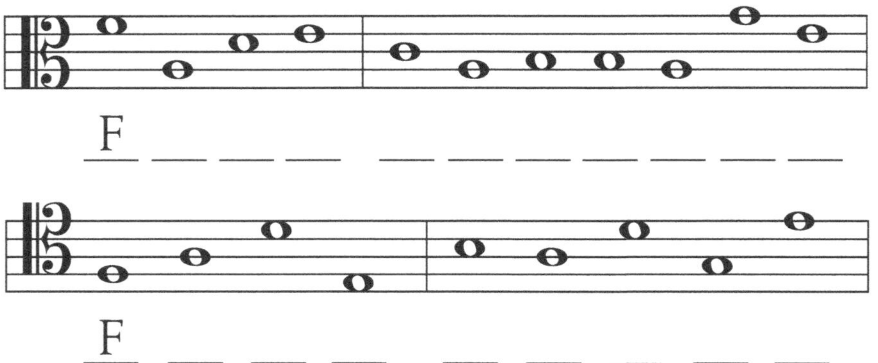

PROJECT: CREATE YOUR OWN CLEF

Using a five line staff, design and draw your own original clef sign. Name your clef and decide which note your clef will designate. Spell 3 words using the line and space notes of your clef. Exchange your clef with a partner. Can you read the words spelled on your partner's clef?

SOME THINGS TO CONSIDER

When and why would a composer choose to use a clef other than treble or bass? Which clef do you find easiest to read? Why? Do you like to read notes on ledger lines? Why or why not? Could changing the clef sign eliminate the need for ledger lines? Discuss these questions with the class.

HALF STEPS, WHOLE STEPS, MAJOR SCALE

Name _______________________________________

A **half step** is the smallest distance between two keys on the piano. It is also the smallest interval commonly used in western music.

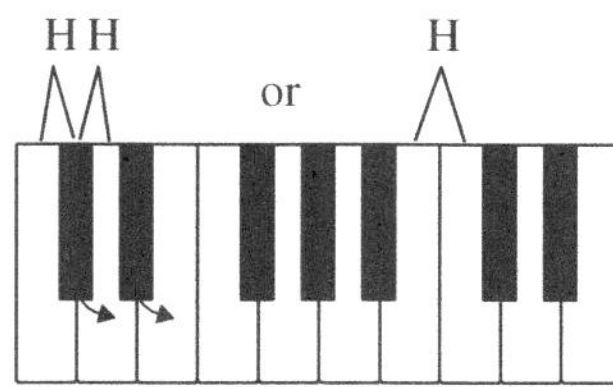

On the piano most half steps are between a black key and a white key. There are two places where a half step occurs between white keys: E-F, and B-C.

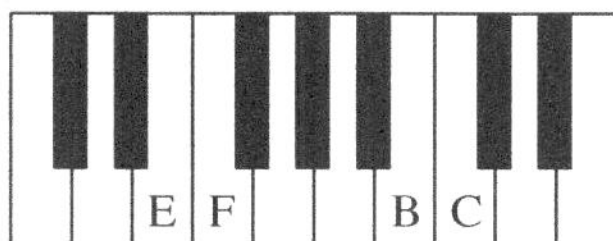

A **whole step** is a combination of two half steps side by side on the keyboard. A whole step on the piano keyboard can be between two white keys, two black keys, or a black and a white key.

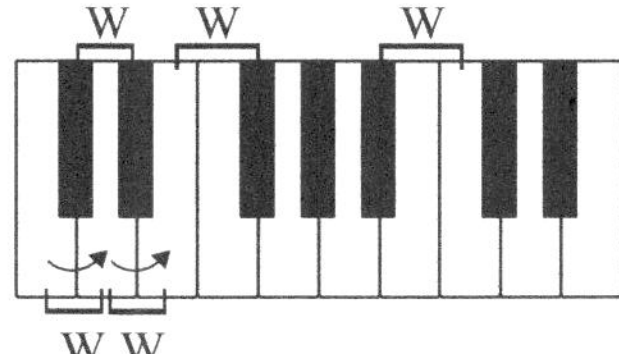

HALF OR WHOLE?

Circle H (half step) or W (whole step) for each of the keyboards below. Play each example on a keyboard or other instruments in your classroom.

1. 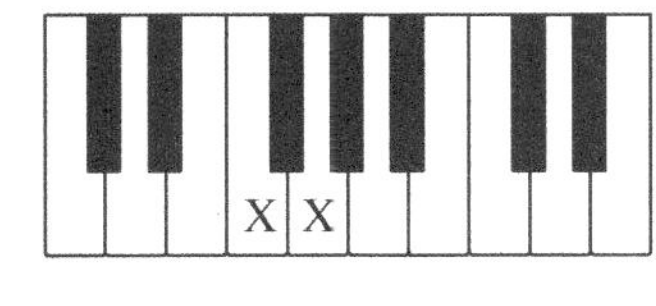

    H   W

2. 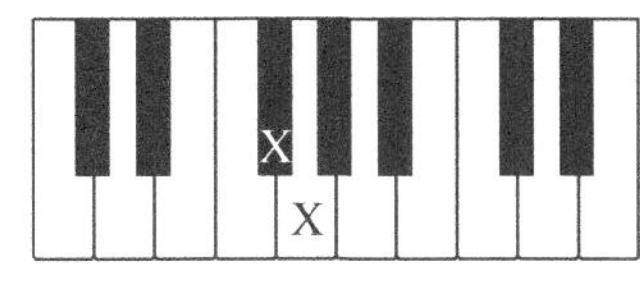

    H   W

3. 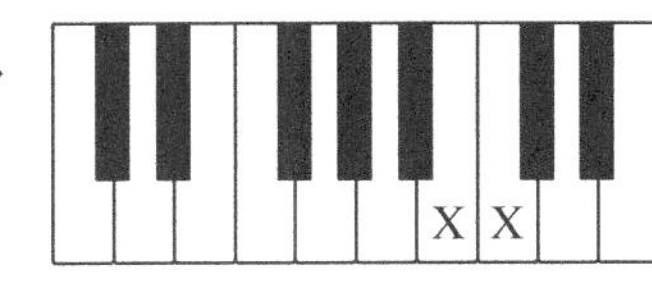

    H   W

4. 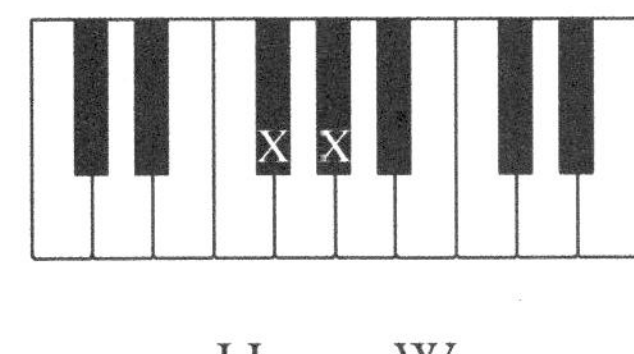

    H   W

5. 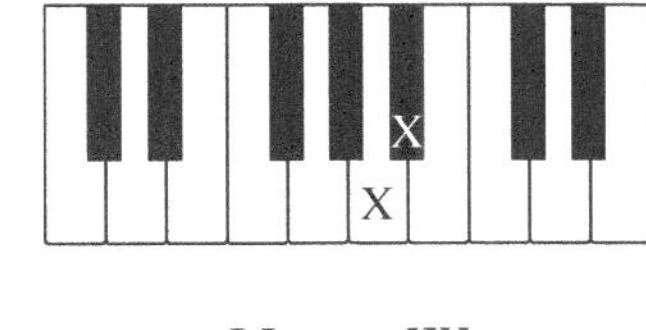

    H   W

6. 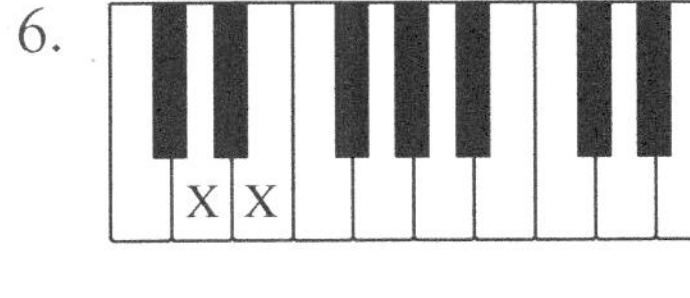

    H   W

A **scale** is a set of pitches in an arrangement of whole and half steps. The word scale comes from the Italian word *scala*, meaning ladder. Like a ladder, the pitches of a scale are arranged from lowest to highest, (ascending) or highest to lowest (descending). One of the most common and familiar scales is the **major scale**. The major scale uses a specific arrangement of half and whole steps to give it its distinctive sound: **W W H W W W H**

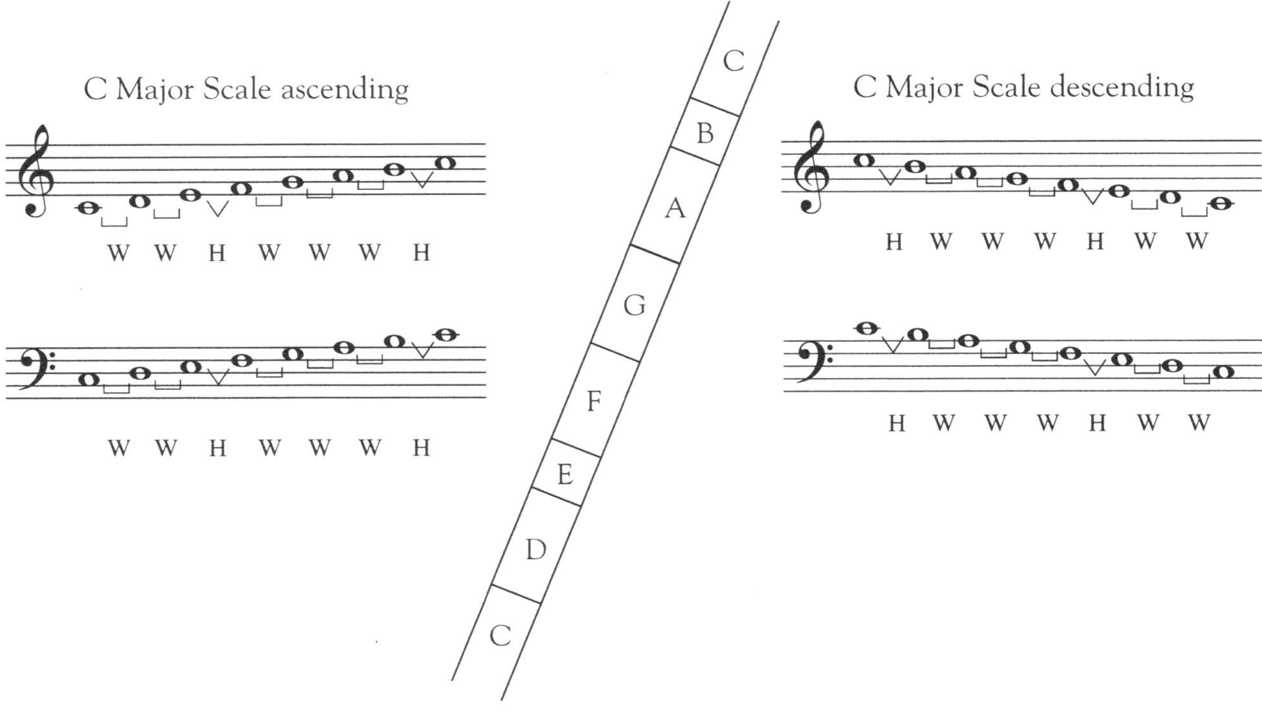

CLIMB THE C SCALE

Draw the C major scale on each staff below. Write the pitch names beneath each note and then mark the whole and half steps. Play or sing each scale.

PROJECT: VOCABULARY QUIZ

Write the letter of the word by its definition below.

a. staff	b. clef
c. pitch	d. brace
e. treble clef	f. bass clef
g. ledger	h. half step
i. whole step	j. scale
k. scala	l. ascending
m. descending	n. alto clef

______set of pitches in a specific arrangement of half and whole steps

______line used to connect treble and bass clef to form a grand staff

______short lines used to extend the staff higher or lower

______scale notes arranged from highest to lowest

______symbol used to designate the third line of a staff as middle C

______symbol used to identify F as the 4th line on the staff

______Italian word meaning ladder

______5 horizontal lines and 4 spaces used to notate music

______highness or lowness of sound

______symbol at the beginning of the staff that determines the pitch names for that staff

______two half steps side by side on a keyboard

______symbol used to identify G as the 2nd line on the staff

______smallest interval in western music, smallest distance between two keys on a piano

______scale notes arranged from lowest to highest

INTERVALS

Name _______________________________

An **interval** in music is the distance between two notes and is identified by a number. To find the distance or interval between two notes, count the number of lines and spaces between the notes, <u>including the note you start on and the note you end on</u>. Play or sing each of the intervals on the treble clef below.

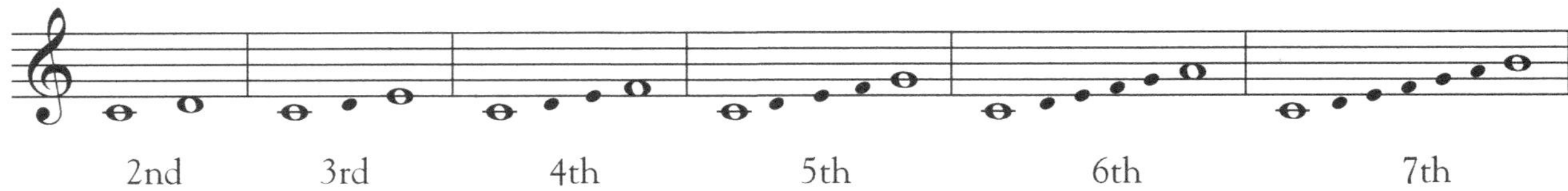

Add a note to show these intervals on the bass staff below. The first one has been done for you.

When two notes are the same interval, it is called **prime**, or **unison**. An interval of 8 notes is called an **octave**.

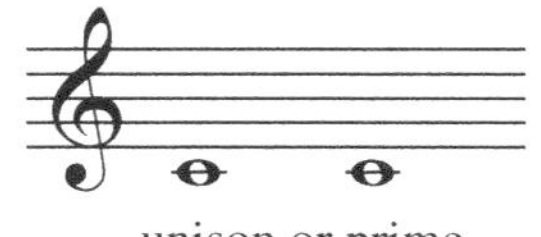

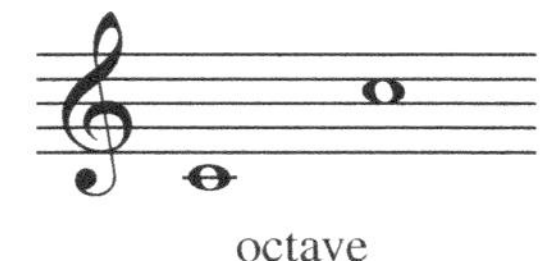

WHAT'S YOUR INTERVAL?

Identify the following intervals. With a partner or in small groups, sing each interval or play the intervals on a keyboard. Take turns identifying the intervals by ear.

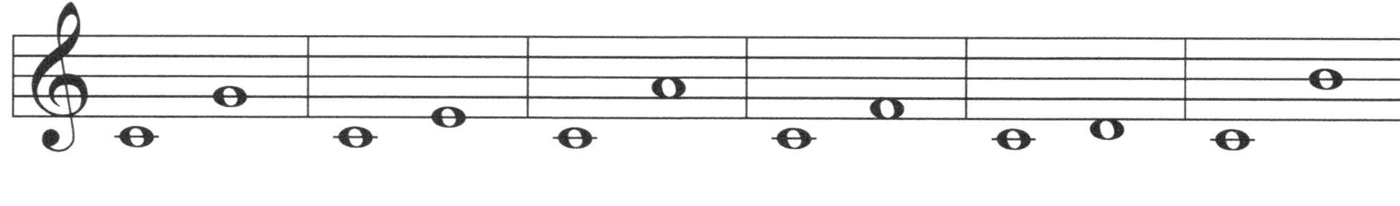

OTHER INTERVAL FACTS

Intervals can be classified as **melodic** or **harmonic**. Melodic intervals occur between notes played one after the other. Harmonic intervals occur when notes are played at the same time. **Simple intervals** are those within an octave. **Compound intervals** are those larger than an octave.

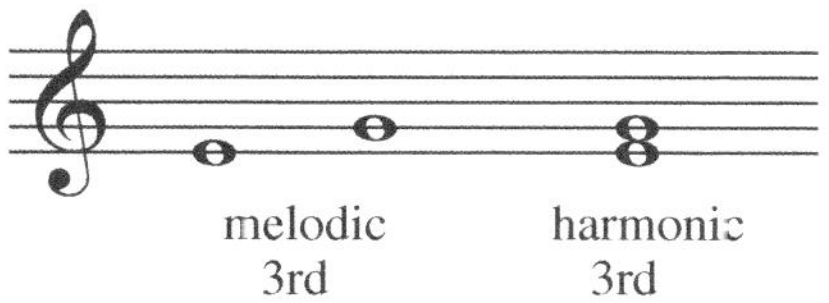

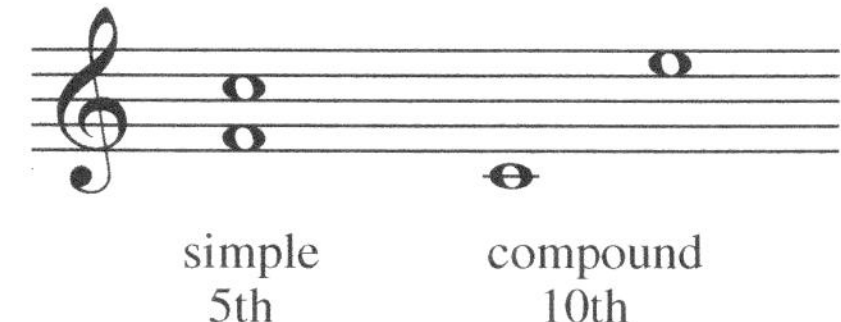

PROJECT: INTERVAL CLASSIFICATION

Complete the chart below. The first interval is done as an example.

Interval	Name	Melodic or Harmonic?	Simple or Compound?
	2nd	harmonic	simple

CHALLENGE: INTERVAL DICTATION

Notate the following intervals on the staves below, first treble clef then bass clef. You may start on any pitch for each example. You may wish to use ledger lines for some of the intervals.

1. melodic 2nd

2. harmonic 4th

3. melodic 7th

4. harmonic 3rd

5. harmonic 2nd

6. melodic 6th

7. harmonic unison

8. melodic 10th

9. melodic octave

10. harmonic 5th

SHARP, FLAT, NATURAL

Name ____

Placing a **sharp** in front of a note raises the pitch a half step. Add sharps to these treble clef notes. Be sure to place the sharp sign in *front* of the note. The "center square" of the sharp sign includes the line or space of the note.

Placing a **flat** in front of a note lowers the pitch a half step. Add flat signs to these bass clef notes. Place the round part of the flat sign carefully to include the line or space of the note.

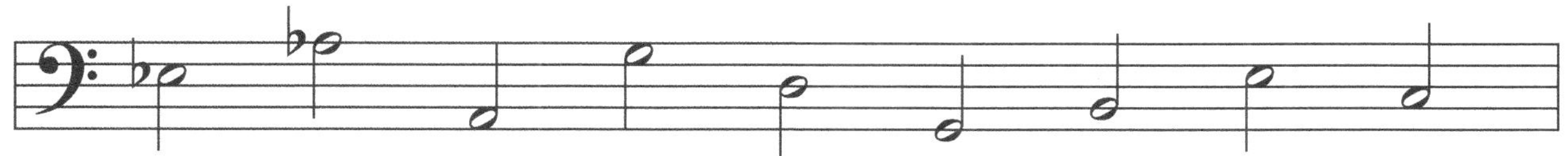

The black keys on the piano get their name from the white keys.

When going "up the scale," the black keys have "sharp" names.

When going "down the scale," the black keys have "flat" names.

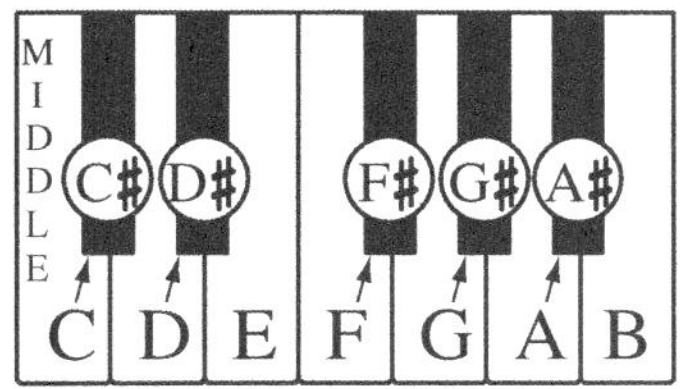

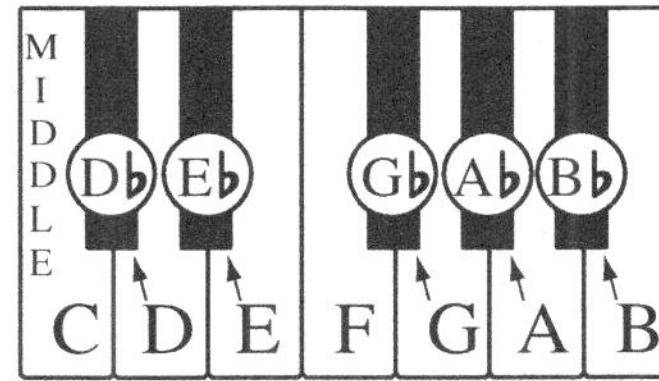

Circle these keys on the keyboard: A♯, D♯, G♯, D♭, E♭.

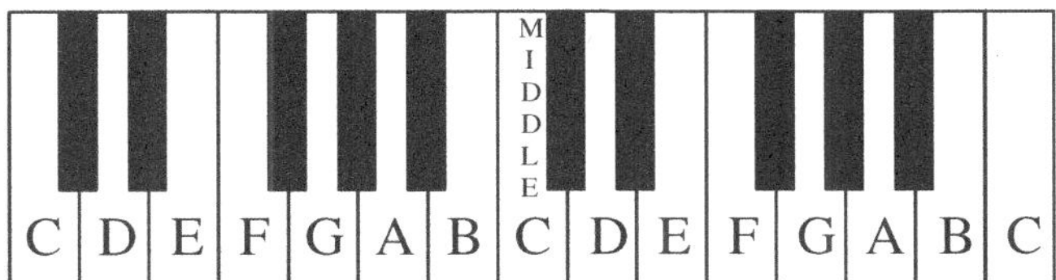

SHARPS AND FLATS IN THE TREBLE CLEF

Name the following sharp and flat pitches.

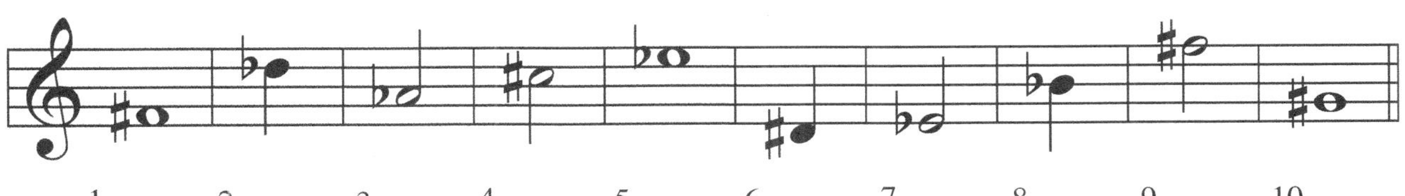

1. ____ 2. ____ 3. ____ 4. ____ 5. ____ 6. ____ 7. ____ 8. ____ 9. ____ 10. ____

SHARPS AND FLATS IN THE BASS CLEF

Name the following sharp and flat pitches.

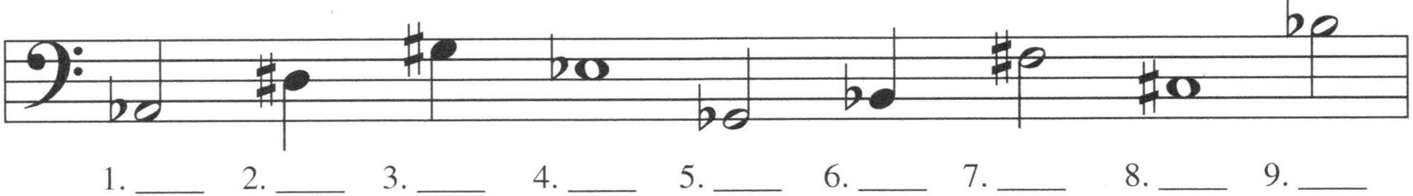

1. ___ 2. ___ 3. ___ 4. ___ 5. ___ 6. ___ 7. ___ 8. ___ 9. ___

HOW LONG?

Notes that are sharp or flat stay sharp or flat for an entire measure. A **natural sign** is used to cancel a sharp or flat. Add a natural sign to the second note in each measure below to cancel the sharp or flat.

PROJECT: CONSTRUCTION ZONE

Construct the following musical excerpt by following the steps given.

1. Complete the grand staff by adding treble and bass clefs in both lines.
2. Add a 3/4 time signature.
3. Finish drawing bar lines.
4. Draw a flat in front of all the Bs.
5. Draw a sharp in front of the last 2 Fs in the treble clef.
6. Draw a flat in front of the Es in the bass clef.

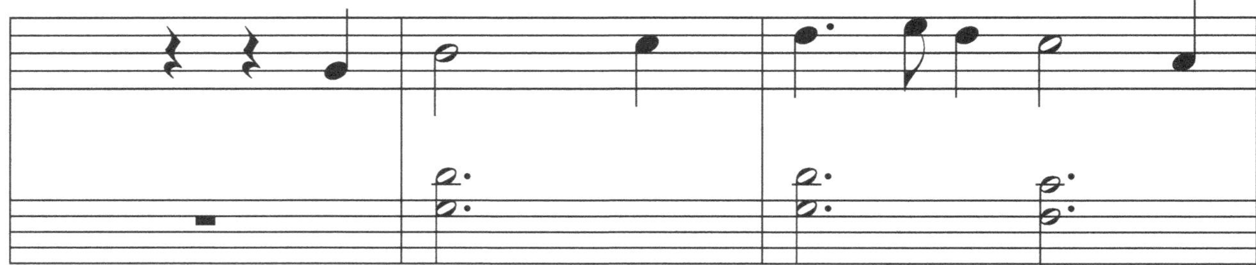

CHALLENGE

Play this musical excerpt. Can you name the song it comes from?

KEY SIGNATURE

Name _______________________________

Sharps or flats placed immediately to the right of the clef sign are called the **key signature**. These symbols affect every note named by the sharps or flats for the entire song. When sharps or flats appear in a key signature it is no longer necessary to place them next to each individual note.

In the example below, every F is now raised a half step to F♯ because of the F♯ in the key signature.

In the next example every B is now lowered a half step to B♭ because of the B♭ in the key signature.

Name the flats in the key signature below. ______ ______ ______
Circle the notes that would be played flat.

Name the sharps in the key signature below. ______ ______
Circle the notes that would be played sharp.

There are **15 different key signatures**: 7 sharp keys, 7 flat keys, and one key that has no sharps or flats, the key of C.

SHARP KEY SIGNATURES

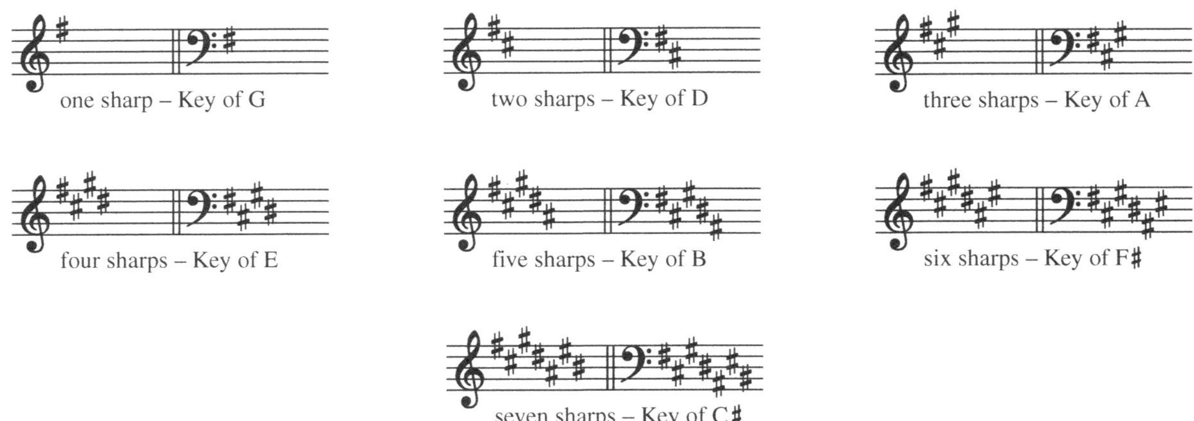

SHARP KEYS

An easy way to find the name of a sharp key signature is to count up one half step from the last sharp (farthest to the right). For example:

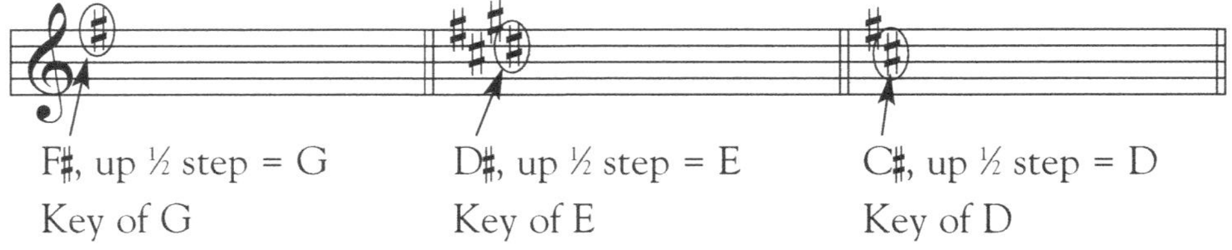

NAME THAT SHARP KEY!

Each key signature names the key of the piece. For example, a song in the Key of E uses the pitches of the E scale. The sharped pitches are F, C, G, D.

Use the key signatures to name each of these major keys. Draw the scale of that key on the staff and fill in note names.

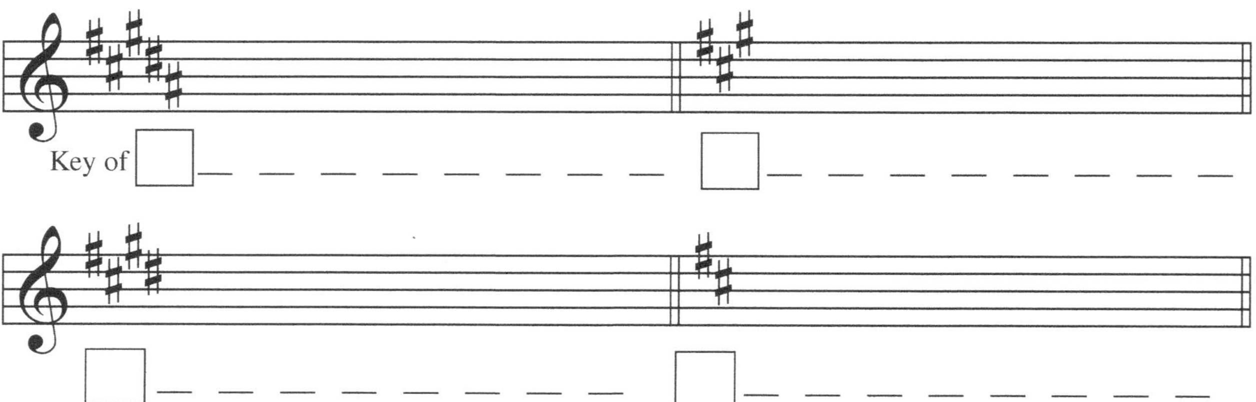

FLAT KEY SIGNATURES

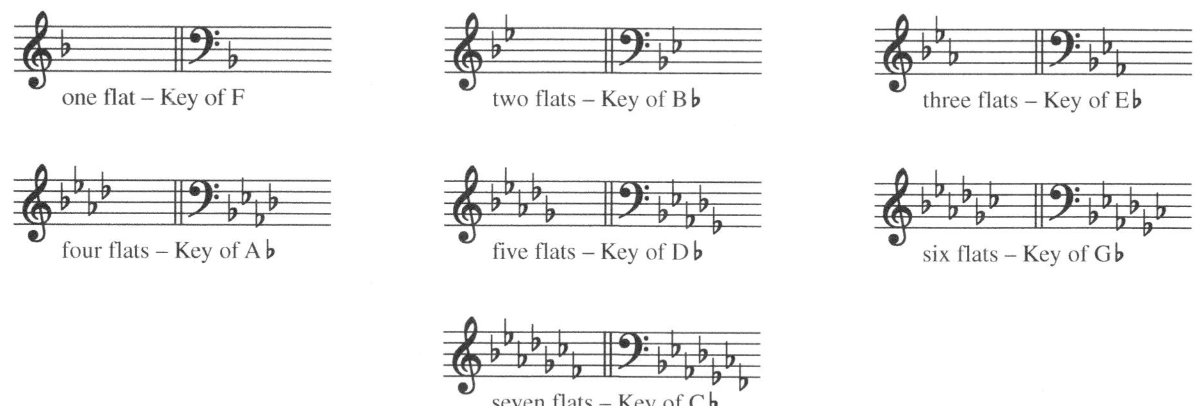

FLAT KEYS

An easy way to determine the name of a flat key signature is to name the second to last flat from the right. Except for the key of F (only one flat), all of the flat keys have "flat" in their name.

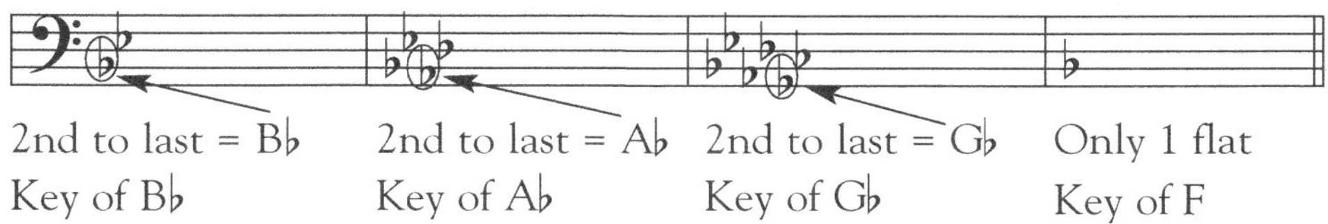

NAME THAT FLAT KEY!

Use the key signatures to name each of these major keys. Draw the scale of that key on the staff and fill in note names.

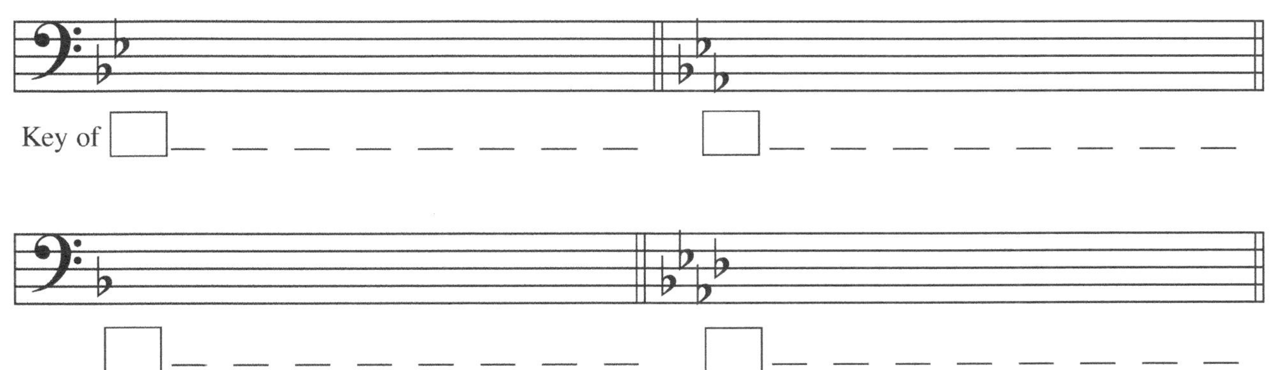

KEY OF C (no sharps or flats)

Draw the C scale below and fill in note names.

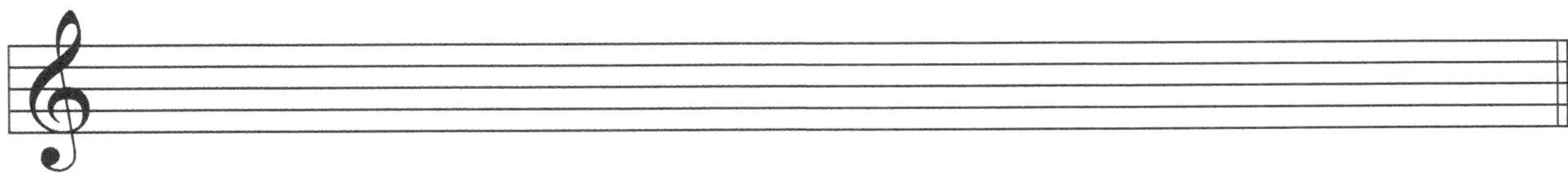

PROJECT: KEY MATCH-UP!

Draw a line to connect each key signature to its key name.

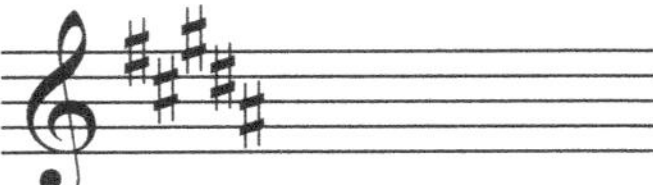

D Major

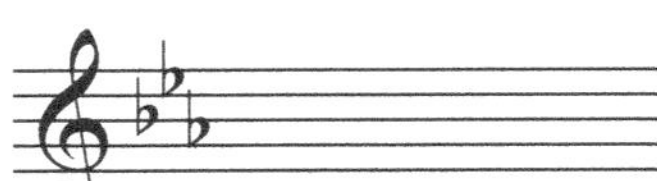

A Major

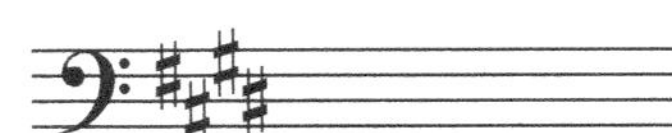

E♭ Major

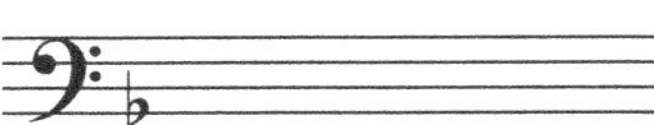

D♭ Major

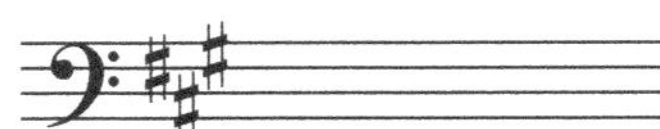

E Major

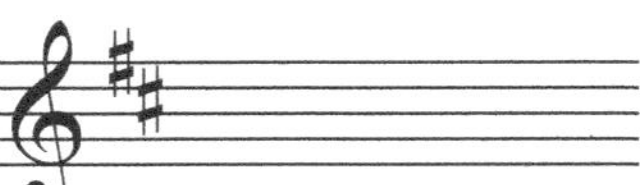

B Major

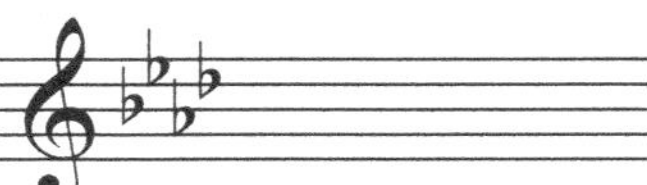

G Major

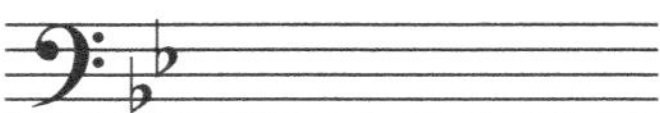

C Major

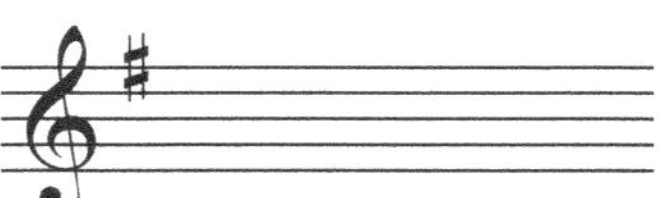

F Major

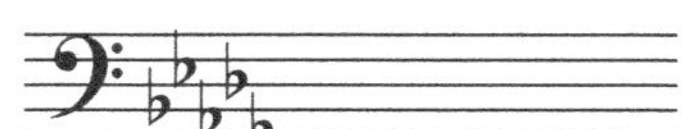

C♯ Major

A♭ Major

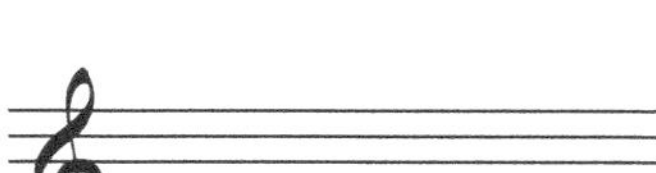

B♭ Major

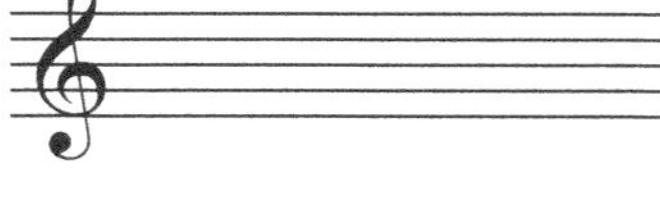

F♯ Major

MORE SCALES

Name ____

Each major scale has a **relative minor scale** that shares the same key signature. The term *relative* is used because that is how the two scales are related, by their shared key signature. The relative minor scale begins on the 6th step of the major scale with the same key signature.

A minor	A	B	C	D	E	F	G	A
	1	2	3	4	5	6	7	8

C major	C	D	E	F	G	A	B	C
	1	2	3	4	5	6	7	8

Minor scales are unique in that they have 3 forms: **Natural**, **Harmonic**, and **Melodic**.

NATURAL MINOR

When the scale begins on A and uses the C Major key signature (no sharps or flats), it is called the A natural minor scale. Notice that a new pattern of half and whole steps is created: W H W W H W W. Play this scale.

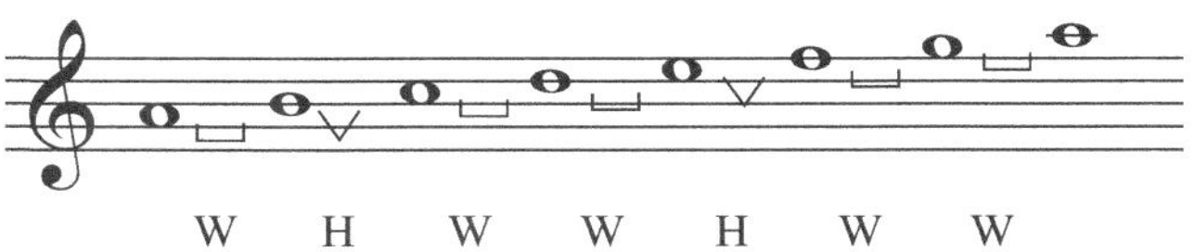

HARMONIC MINOR

Raise the 7th pitch of the scale ascending and descending. NOTE: When you raise the 7th step, the distance between steps 6 and 7 becomes one and one-half steps. (W+H) Play this scale.

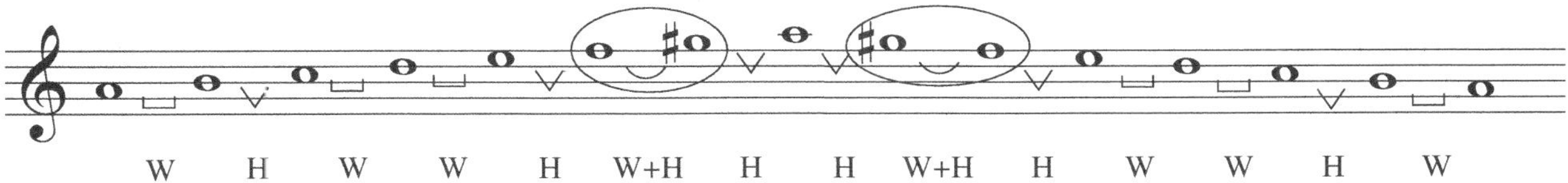

MELODIC MINOR

Raise the 6th and 7th pitches of the scale ascending, <u>but not descending</u>. Play this scale.

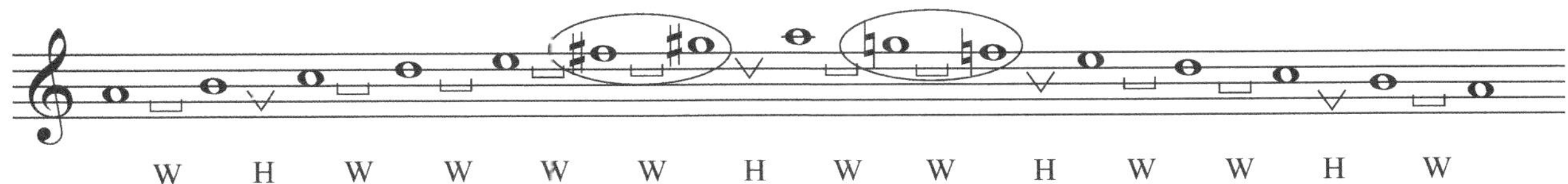

MAJOR OR MINOR?

Name each of the scales below. Then decide if the scale is major or minor. If it is minor, decide which form: natural, harmonic or melodic. Circle your answer. Finally, mark in the half (H) and whole (W) steps.

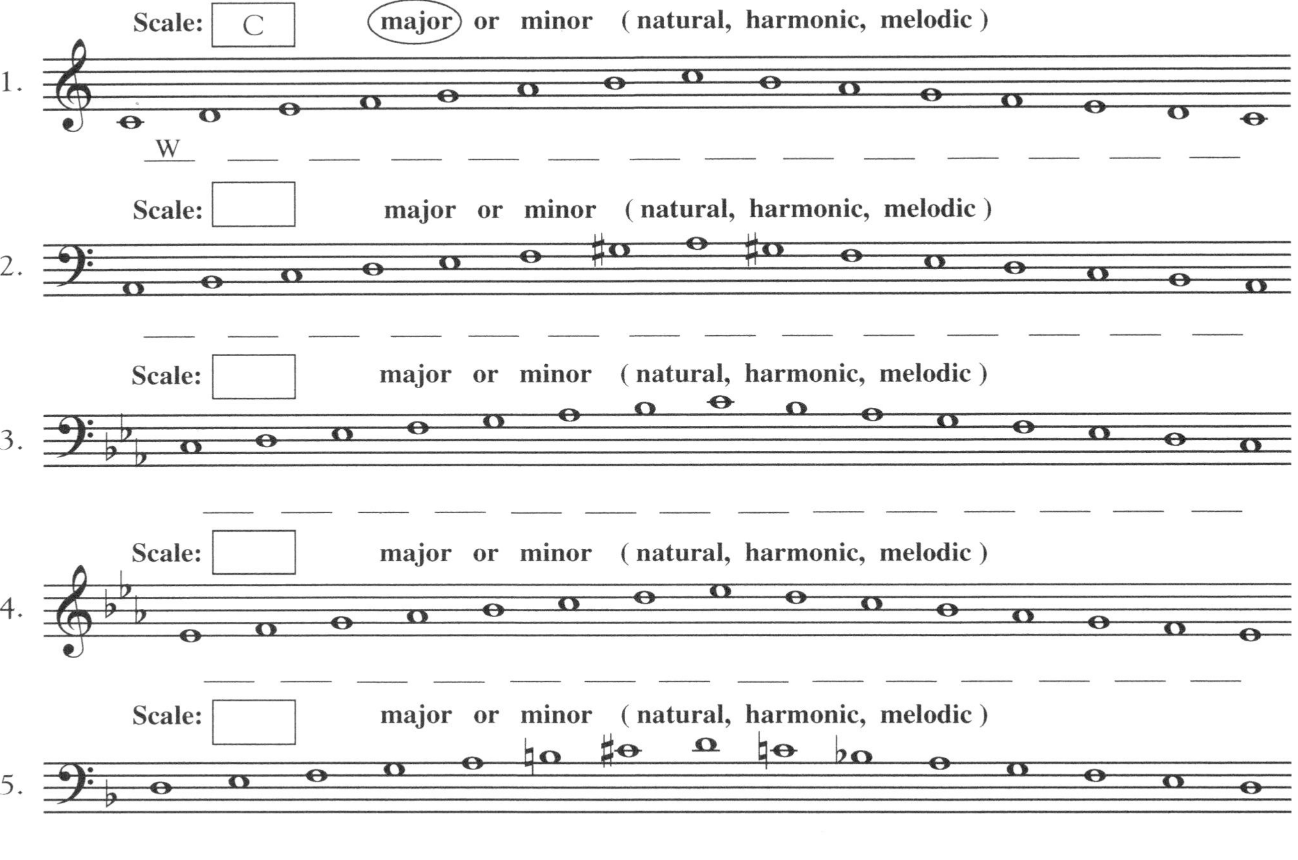

CHROMATIC SCALE

A **chromatic scale** is made up of 12 consecutive half steps. It can begin on any note. Chromatic scales going up (ascending) use sharps; chromatic scales going down (descending) use flats.

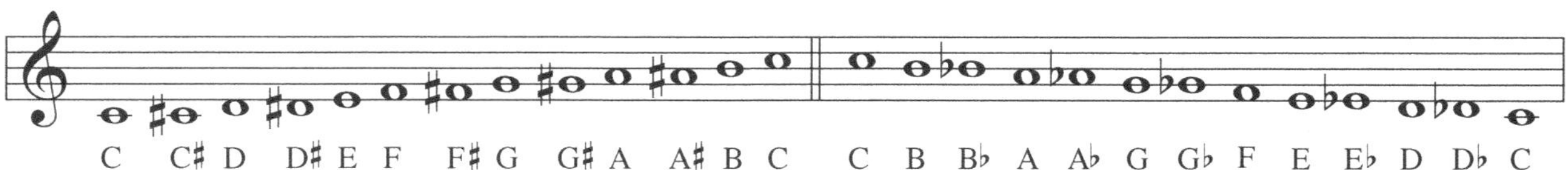

Notate the following chromatic scales.

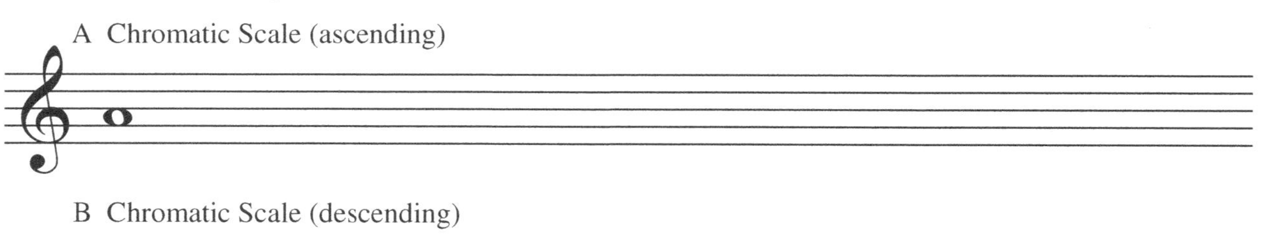

WHOLE TONE SCALE

A **whole tone scale** uses a pattern of 7 consecutive whole steps. This scale can begin on any note and has an exotic sound. Write a whole tone scale on the bass clef and mark the whole steps. Play both scales.

BLUES SCALE

The **blues scale** is heard in blues and jazz. The interval pattern for this scale is:

W+H   W   H   H   W+H   W

Notate the blues scale on the treble clef. Mark the intervals.

PROJECT: CHOOSE YOUR SCALE

Choose two of the following scales: major, natural minor, harmonic minor, melodic minor, chromatic, whole tone, and blues. Notate the scale ascending and descending. Use a key signature or add sharps or flats as needed. Mark the pattern of half and whole steps below the notes.

1. scale name_____________________

2. scale name_____________________

CHALLENGE

Can you sing the scales you notated?

ELEMENTS OF MELODY QUIZ

Name ____

Name the pitches on the treble staff.

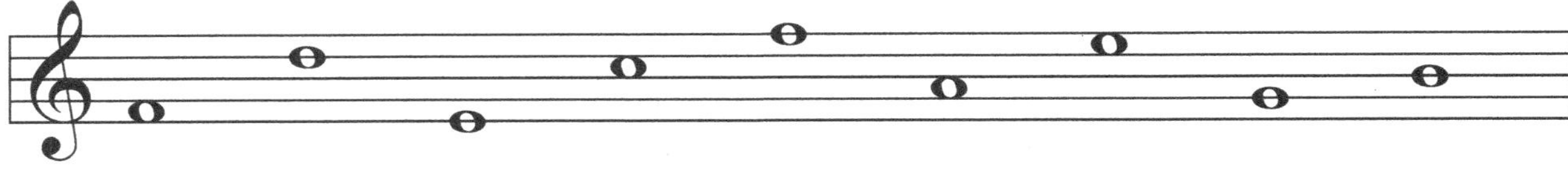

Name the pitches on the bass staff.

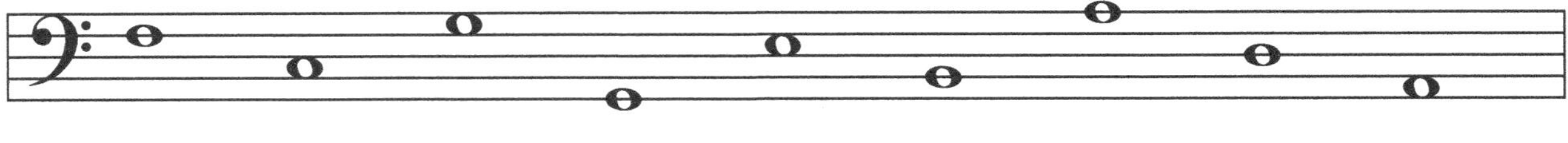

Name the pitches on the ledger lines.

Mark an X on the keyboard to show the half or whole step above each pitch given on the keyboard. The first one has been done for you.

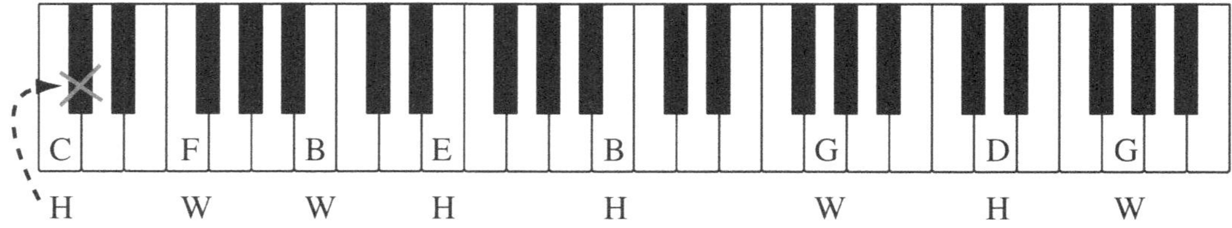

Use "M" for melodic and "H" for harmonic and identify the following intervals with their name and number. The first one has been done for you.

Notate the melodic (M) and harmonic (H) intervals. Begin on any pitch.

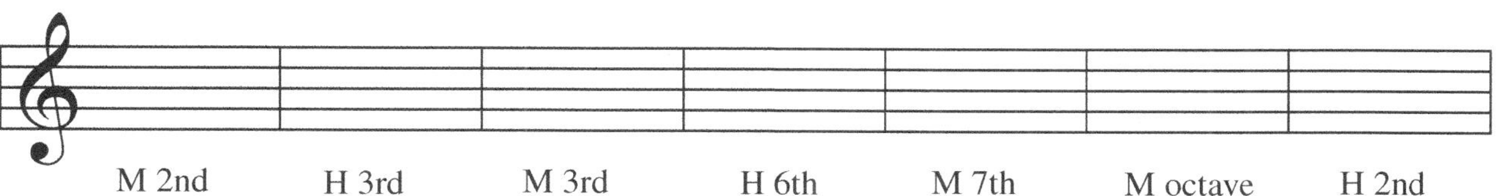

| M 2nd | H 3rd | M 3rd | H 6th | M 7th | M octave | H 2nd |

| H 4th | H 5th | H 7th | M 6th | M 5th | M 4th | H unison |

Name the major key signatures. Notate each major scale ascending.
Label the half and whole steps.

1. ________

2. ________

3. ________

4. ________

TRUE OR FALSE?

T F ♯ = sharp

T F ♭ = natural

T F 𝄡 = moveable clef

T F A natural sign cancels every flat and sharp in the piece.

T F Melodic is a form of minor scale.

T F A chromatic scale uses a pattern of H and W steps.

T F The key of C has no sharps and no flats.

ACCIDENTALS, ENHARMONIC NOTES

Name ____

A sharp, flat or natural placed before a note that is not in the key signature is called an **accidental**. When an accidental appears, every note that follows it on the same line or space in that measure is also changed by the accidental. After the barline, the accidental is cancelled.

TIME FOR A CHANGE

Name the accidentals. The first one has been done for you.

An exception to this is when a note with an accidental is tied over a barline. Then the accidental holds through to the next measure.

In addition to sharp, flat and natural, there are two other symbols used to alter notes. **Double sharp** 𝄪 raises a note a whole step. **Double flat** ♭♭ lowers a note a whole step.

Notes that sound the same but have different names are called **enharmonic notes**. For example, C♯ and D♭ sound the same but have different names.

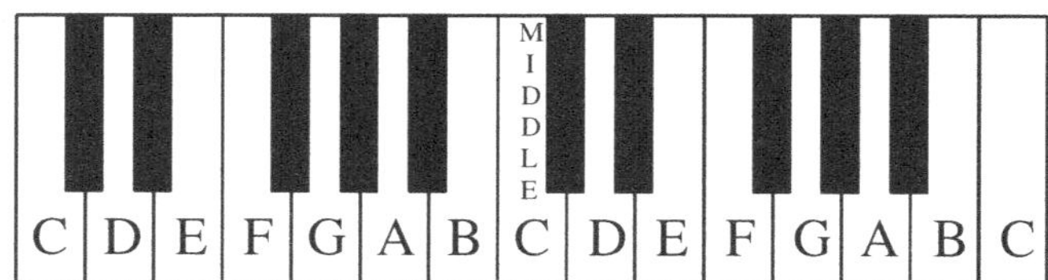

Using the keyboard above, locate and name these enharmonic notes.

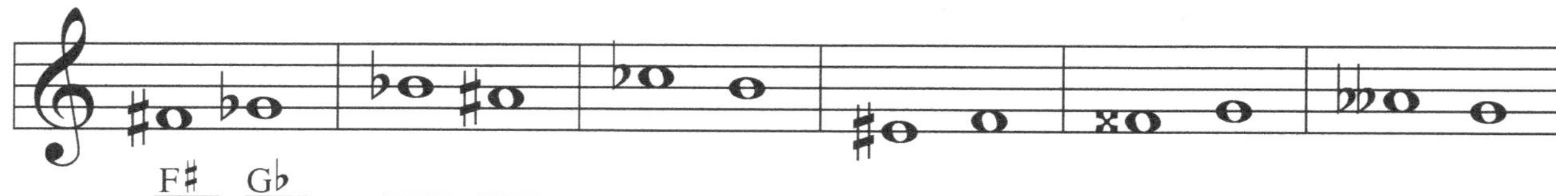

ENHARMONIC NOTATION

Notate the enharmonic for each pitch on the staff. You may need to use: ♯, ♭, ♮, 𝄪, 𝄫,

E   F♭   __   __   __   __   __   __   __   __

PROJECT: ASK THE COMPOSER

In the music excerpt below, notice the key signature and study the circled notes. Answer the question for each corresponding circled note.

1. Name the key signature. Which notes will be sharped throughout?

    ________________________   ________________

2. Is this sharp an accidental? ________________

3. What is the name of this note? ______________

4. Name this accidental. Will it be played on the keyboard as a white or a black key?

    ________________________   ________________

5. What previous accidental is this natural canceling? ______________

6. Is this sharp found in the key signature? ________________

7. Is this natural sign canceling a previous accidental? ____________

8. Name this accidental. Can a flat be used when there are sharps in the key signature?

    ________________________   ________________

9. Why is there a sharp sign in front of this note? ________________________________

10. What previous accidental is this natural canceling? ________________

from "Rock-a-My Soul"
American Folk Songs and Spirituals,
Hal Leonard Corporation

TEMPO

Name ____

Tempo is an Italian word meaning time. In music, tempo means how fast or slow the steady beat is counted. Found at the beginning of a piece of music above the time signature, tempo has been traditionally written in Italian. In more modern times the use of English to describe tempo has become more frequent. Some common Italian tempo indications include:

largo: very slow

andante: "walking" pace

allegretto: moderately fast

vivace: lively

adagio: slow

moderato: moderate

allegro: quickly, fast

presto: very fast

TEMPO WORD SEARCH

Find the tempo indications listed below in this word search puzzle. Look up the meaning of any words you do not know.

adagio

allegro

allegretto

andante

andantino

grave

largo

lento

moderato

presto

prestissimo

vivace

```
P J X U O W C X E M Q Q I C X A S
K V A M L A D A G I O A Z C E L I
Z U O P U E P N M P A N M J A L I
O P F I R A N P E U N D O I S E T
U R I L D E T T Q J D A D G O G T
U E I F C F S D O J A N E H Q R Y
X S B N E O O T D Z N T R A C E G
Z T E V G C N N I O T I A L P T B
U O V U I B I G G S E N T L L T M
E Z F T O V Q R H J S O O E T O G
R Y O R W X A F C Y T I Q G I P H
P M N O Q L V C M T E U M R K L W
S G O S L V B C E V N C X O T Q M
P C C G R A V E P I D A K C M Z O
```

Often other descriptive words are added to the basic tempo indication to give the performer a greater sense of the character and style of the music. Some of these include:

molto: much, very

non troppo: not too much

poco a poco: little by little

meno: less

Tempo does not always stay the same throughout an entire piece of music. **Accelerando** (accel.) means to gradually increase the tempo, while **ritardando** (rit.) means to gradually slow the tempo down.

TEMPO TRANSLATION

Write the meanings of the following Italian tempo indications in English.

*molto vivace*____

allegro non troppo ____

acccelerando poco a poco ____

molto ritardando ____

Tempo indications can give an approximate idea of speed and character. Each musician will interpret them in his or her own way. For example, your idea of andante, ("walking" pace) may be different than your classmate's andante. In 1816 Johann Maelzel began manufacturing the **metronome**, which at that time was a pendulum-like instrument that could produce a steady "ticking" beat at various speeds. Today metronomes can be wound with a key, run on electricity, or are battery powered. Metronomes allow a composer to specify exactly how fast or slow a composition is to be played.

PROJECT: CHOOSE THE TEMPO

For each of the songs below, write an Italian or English tempo marking.

1. Oh, Susanna ____

2. America the Beautiful ____

3. Chopsticks ____

4. This Land Is Your Land ____

5. When the Saints Go Marching In ______________________________________

DYNAMICS

Name ____

Dynamics are the degrees of loud and soft in music. They are usually indicated by Italian words and can also be notated using symbols. You may be familiar with many dynamic words and symbols. Circle all of the words and symbols you already know.

symbol	Italian	English
p	*piano*	soft
f	*forte*	loud
mp	*mezzo piano*	medium soft
mf	*mezzo forte*	medium loud
pp	*pianissimo*	very soft
ff	*fortissimo*	very loud
<	*crescendo*	become gradually louder
>	*decrescendo*	become gradually softer

ITALIAN SCRAMBLE

Unscramble the Italian dynamic words.

apino ___________________________   rftoe ___________________________

simpsioina ___________________________   mezoz nopai ___________________________

edonccsre ___________________________   ocdrseeecnd ___________________________

smifirotos ___________________________

Music can be expressed through a broad range of dynamics. Some instruments are known for their delicate soft sound, while others are known for their loud ringing sound. When the piano was invented in the early 1770s it was originally called the *pianoforte*, because it could be played both softly and loudly. Today instrument making and technology have greatly expanded the range of musical dynamics from the intimate sounds of a string quartet to the loudly amplified sounds of a rock concert.

LOUD OR SOFT?

Name two instruments known for their soft sound.

____

Name two instruments capable of a loud full sound.

____

Name a piece of music you know that is mostly *piano* or *mezzo piano* throughout.

____

Name a piece of music you know that is mostly *forte* throughout.

____

PROJECT: DYNAMIC CONTROL

Tap or clap the following rhythms with the dynamics indicated.

CHALLENGE

Write your own four measure rhythm. Add dynamics and perform.

ARTICULATION

Name _______________________________

Articulation affects how musical sound is performed. Musical sounds can be smooth and connected to one another, or short and detached. Symbols represent the many types of articulation commonly heard in music.

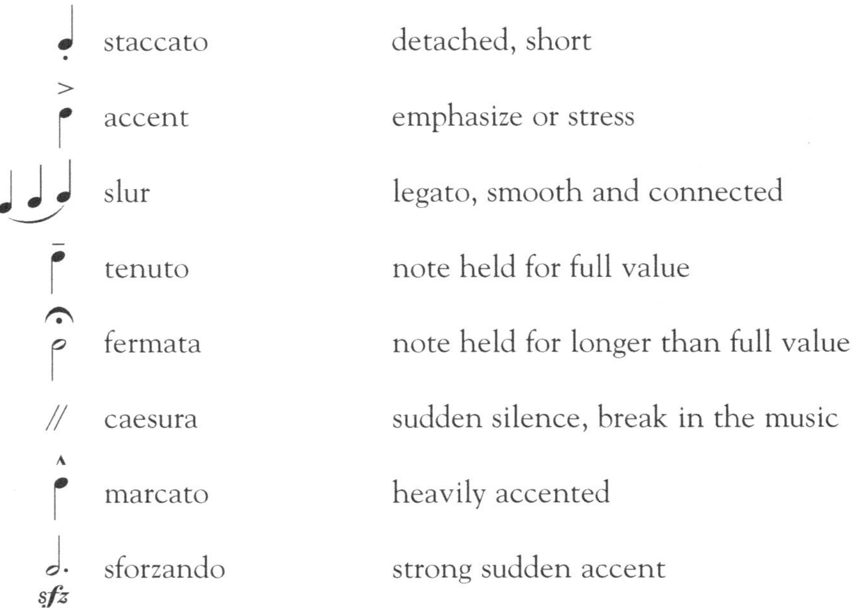

staccato	detached, short
accent	emphasize or stress
slur	legato, smooth and connected
tenuto	note held for full value
fermata	note held for longer than full value
caesura	sudden silence, break in the music
marcato	heavily accented
sforzando	strong sudden accent

ARTICULATION CROSSWORD

Across:

2. stressed note

5. smooth and connected

6. sforzando symbol

7. marcato symbol

Down:

1. sudden break in music

3. note held for full value

4. fermata symbol

5. staccato symbol

SLUR OR TIE?

It's easy to confuse a slur with a tie, the curved line connecting notes of the same pitch. Ties and slurs can be placed above or below a note, and can be long or short, but a tie *always* connects notes of the *same pitch*. Circle tie or slur under each example.

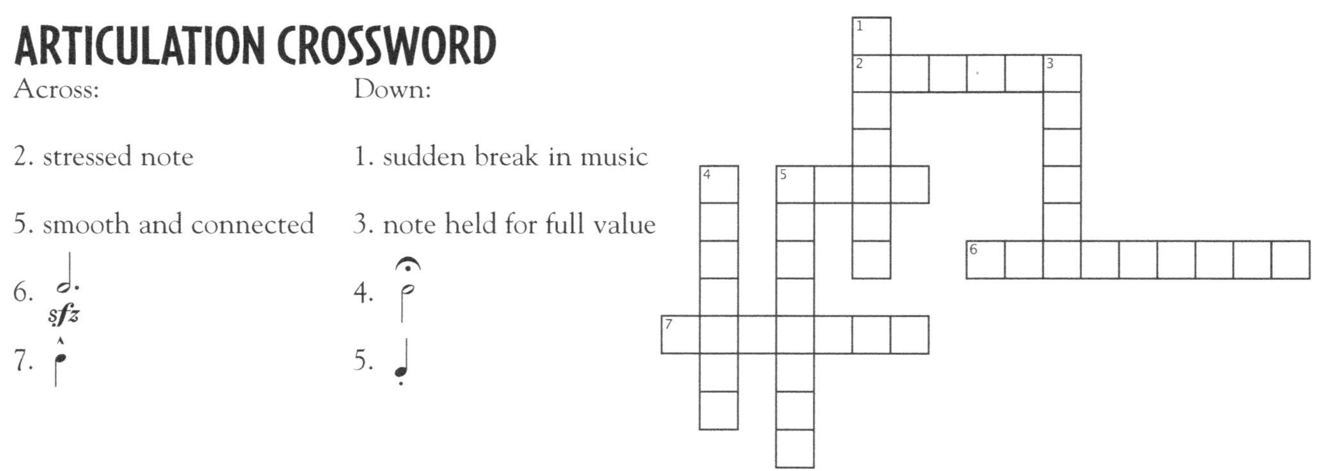

ARTICULATION EXPERIMENT

Try the following with a partner or as a class.

1. Sing "Yankee Doodle" with all the notes staccato

2. Sing "Yankee Doodle" with all the notes legato.

3. Sing "Yankee Doodle" alternating measure of staccato and legato. First measure legato, second measure staccato, third measure legato, etc.

Which of the three ways did you prefer? Why?

PROJECT: WHAT'S YOUR STYLE?

Add the articulation symbols as directed to "Row, Row, Row Your Boat." Perform.

1. Add a slur under the notes in measure 2.

2. Add an accent to both the Es in measure 3.

3. Add staccatos to all the notes in measures 5-6.

4. Add a fermata to the last note in measure 7.

Row, Row, Row Your Boat

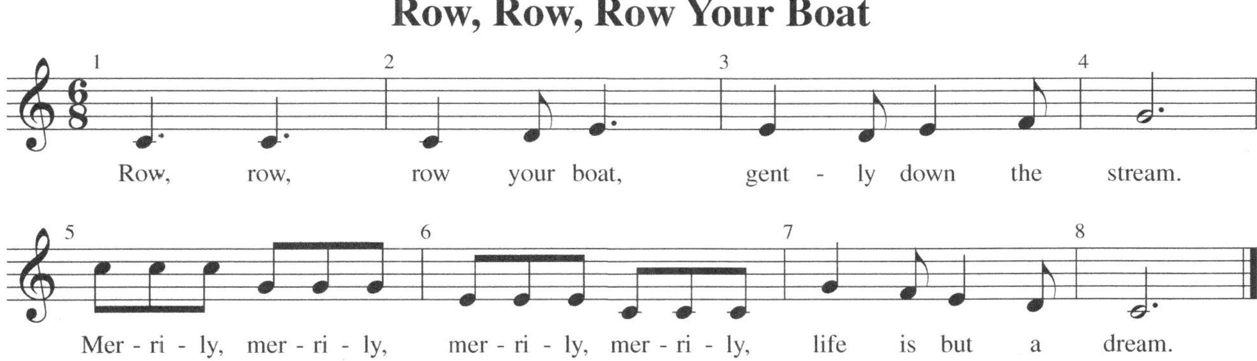

Add at least four articulation symbols of your choice to "Jingle Bells."
Switch with a partner and perform.

Jingle Bells

FORM

Name _______________________________

Form in music is the organization of musical ideas. Pitch, rhythm, dynamics and tempo come together to become a piece of music. Form shows the overall design or shape of a musical composition.

One of the simplest forms in music is **two-part form**, also called **binary** form. A common two-part form is a song with a verse that alternates with a refrain, as in "Jingle Bells." Form is often shown using letters. Two-part form would be AB. "Jingle Bells" is an example of **AB** form.

Verse (A): Dashing through the snow, in a one-horse open sleigh,
O'er the fields we go, laughing all the way!
Bells on bobtail ring, making spirits bright,
What fun it is to ride and sing a sleighing song tonight!

Refrain (B): Jingle bells, jingle bells, jingle all the way.
Oh what fun it is to ride in a one-horse open sleigh, hey!
Jingle bells, jingle bells, jingle all the way,
Oh what fun it is to ride in a one-horse open sleigh!

Another common form in music is **three-part**, or **ternary** form, shown in letters as ABA. "German Folk Song" is an example of three-part form.

Form can become more complex. Each new section is shown with a different letter. Another common form, **Rondo** form alternates new sections with the return of the **A** section. Shown in letters, Rondo form looks like this: **ABACADA**.

FORM IDENTIFICATION

Match the form shown in shapes to the correct form using letters.

○□	ABA	
○□○□	AABAACAA	○ = A
○□△□○	ABAB	□ = B
○○□○□○○△○	ABACADA	△ = C
○□○	AB	◇ = D
○□○△○◇○	ABCBA	

FORM DETAIL

When sections of music are similar, but not exactly the same, letters can still be used to show the form. In this case a small number 1 is placed after the letter to show there is a slight difference. "Greensleeves" is an example of AA' BB'. Circle the measures in A' that are different from A. Circle the measures in B' that are different from B.

PROJECT: FORMULATIONS

Use letters to show the form of the rhythm examples below. Clap the rhythms after you have labeled the form.

REPEATS AND ENDINGS

Symbols are sometime used to indicate places in the music that repeat or skip ahead. These musical "road signs" make the form of the piece clear and easy to read.

REPEAT SIGN

Two dots before a double bar is called a **repeat sign**. In this example, the repeat sign means to go back to the beginning and perform the music again. Clap the example below.

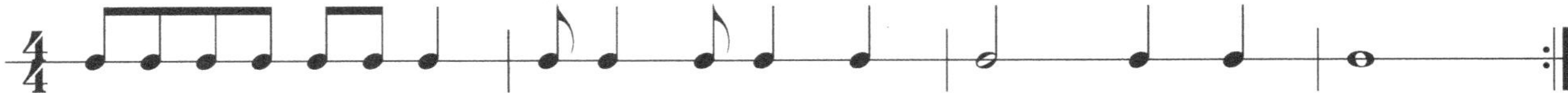

If 2 repeat signs are paired together, repeat only the section of music between the 2 repeat signs.

1ST & 2ND ENDINGS

It is common for a repeated section to end slightly differently the second time, which is indicated by **1st and 2nd ending** signs. Clap through the 1st ending in the example below. Then clap the repeated section, skipping the 1st ending and clapping the 2nd ending.

D.C. AL FINE

D.C. al Fine means return to the beginning and stop at the *Fine* ("the end"). D.C. is the abbreviation for the Italian words *da capo*, meaning "the head." Clap and chant the following example observing the D.C. al Fine.

Skip to My Lou

D.C. AL CODA

D.C. al Coda is Italian for return to the beginning and play to the To Coda ⊕ sign, and then skip to the section marked **coda**. A coda is a separate ending section. (Coda in Italian means "tail," literally a "tail ending!")

D.S. AL CODA

D.S. al Coda means return to the sign 𝄋 and play to the To Coda ⊕ sign, and then skip to the coda. D.S. is the abbreviation for the Italian words *dal segno*, meaning "the sign." Sing "He's Got the Whole World in His Hands," observing the D.S. al Coda.

PROJECT: WHICH WAY DO I GO?

Clap the rhythm below following the symbols given. Then, write out the rhythm as it would appear without any symbols.

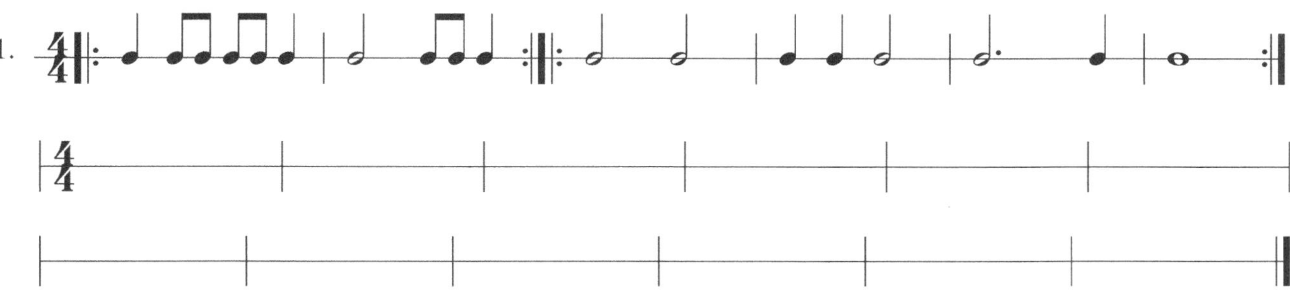

62

TRIADS

Name ____

Melody can be thought of as a group of single notes heard one after another. Harmony can be thought of as groups of notes sounding simultaneously (at the same time). A **triad** is one of the most basic types of harmony. A triad consists of 3 notes played together. For this example below, a triad is built on the first, third and fifth tones of a scale.

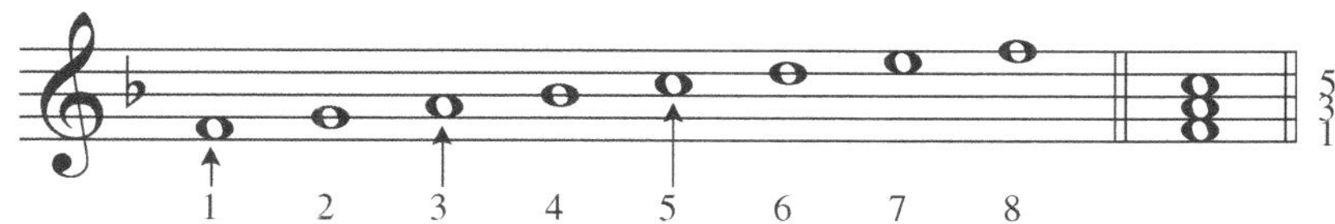

The bottom note of a triad is called the **root**. The triad gets its name from the root. A triad whose root is the first note of a scale is called a **tonic** triad. In addition to being named tonic, it is often labeled with the Roman numeral I. The tonic triad establishes the harmonic center of a piece of music. It is usually found at the beginning of a piece of music, and is almost always found at the end.

TIME FOR TONIC

Circle the first, third and fifth notes in the scale. Write the triad on the staff following the scale. Identify the triad by the name of its root. The first one has been done for you.

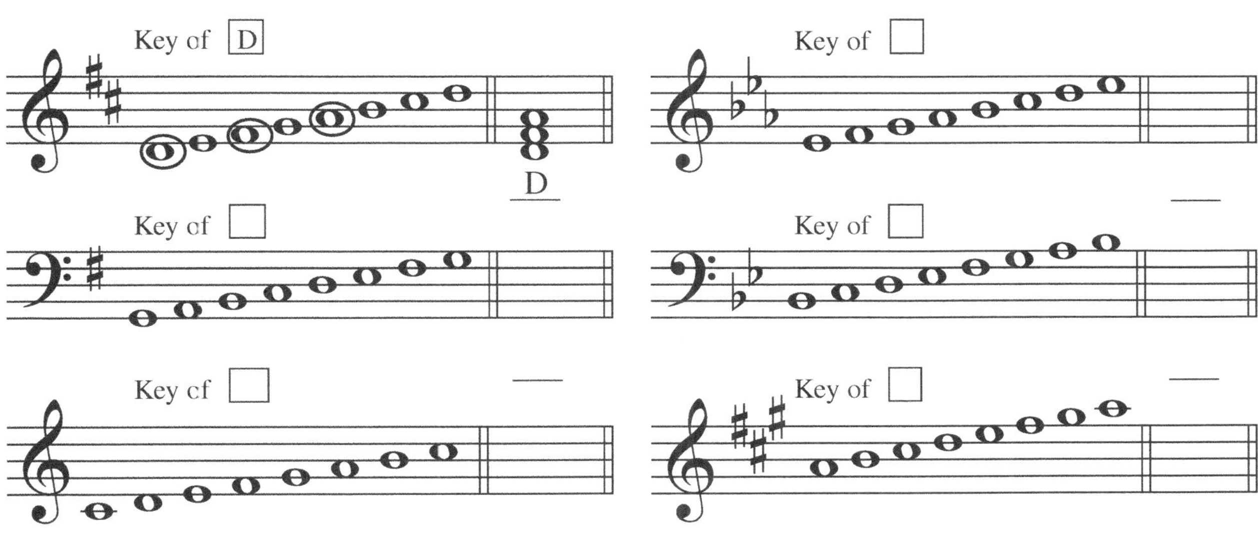

Second in importance to the tonic triad, a **dominant** triad is built on the fifth note of the scale.

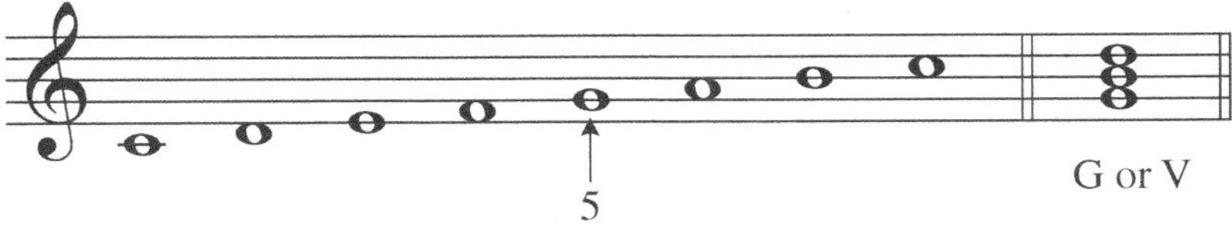

The dominant triad is also named by its root, and is labeled with Roman numeral V, reflecting the fact it begins on the fifth tone of the scale. This chord is closely related to the tonic triad and sets up harmonic tension within the key. Moving from dominant to tonic gives the music a sense of finality. This movement is often heard at the end of a phrase or section. The movement from dominant to tonic is called a **cadence**.

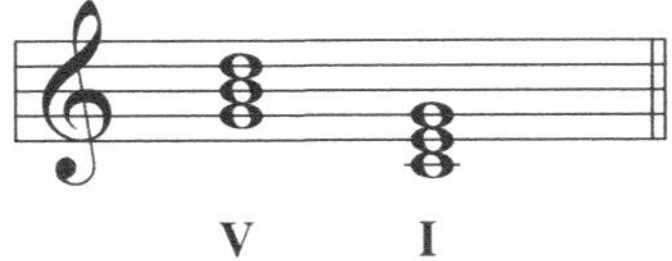

DOMINANT TRIADS

Using the scales given, notate a tonic triad and a dominant triad. Label each with their root name.

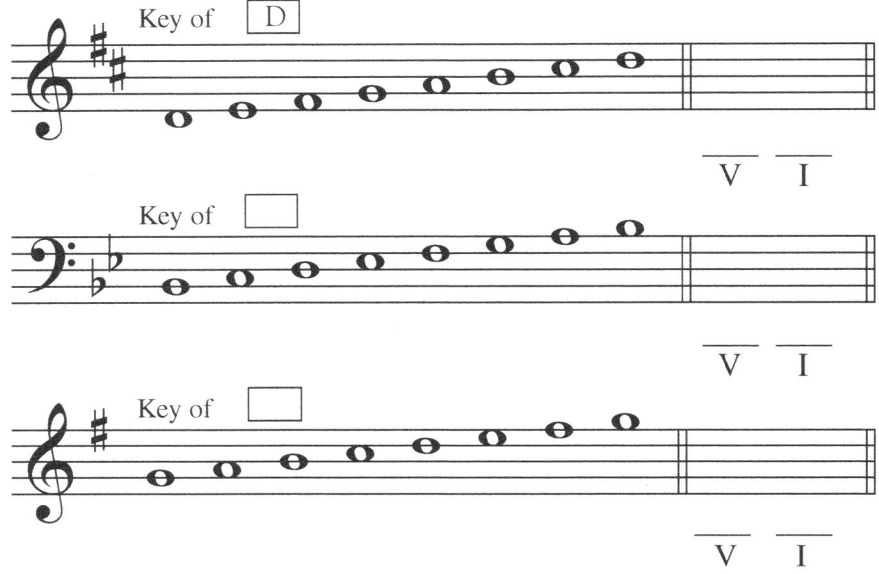

PROJECT: CADENCE DETECTIVE

Identify the following cadences. Name the triads by note name and Roman numeral.

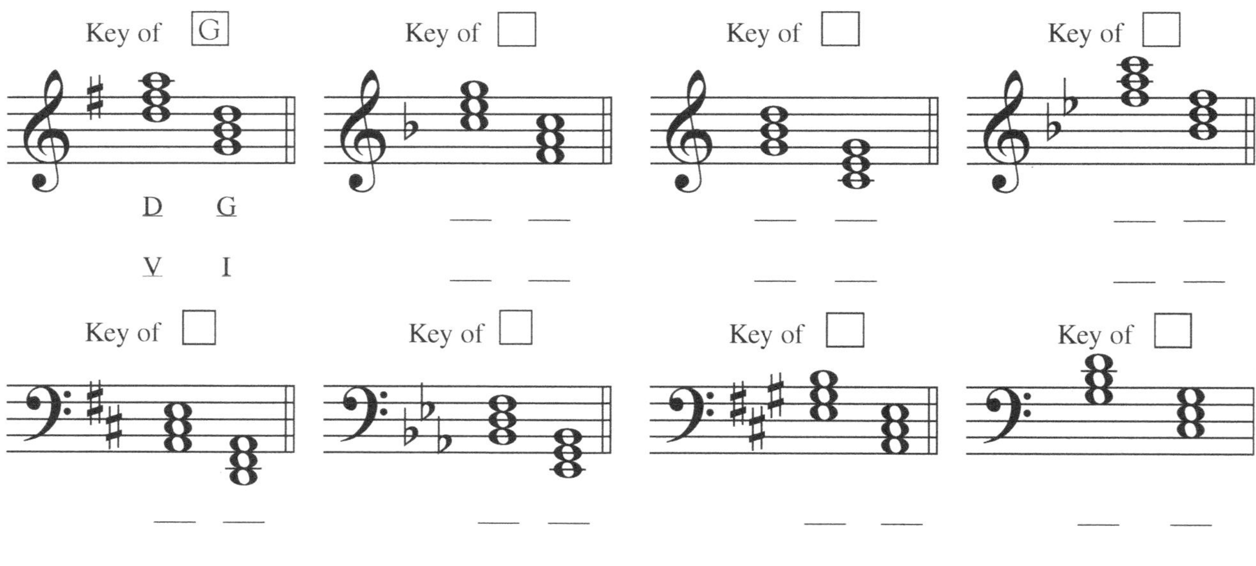

TRANSPOSITION

Name _______________________________

Transposition is changing music in one key to another key. Music is transposed from one key to another for many reasons. The original key of a song may contain notes that are either too high or too low to sing easily. A vocal piece may be transposed to make it easier to play on an instrument. An instrumental piece may be transposed to a key that enables a group of different instruments to play together. Think of at least two more reasons why you might want to change the key of a piece of music.

1. ____

2. ____

TIME TO TRANSPOSE!

In this example, "Mary Had a Little Lamb" is written in the key of F. Number the pitches of the F major scale 1-8. Identify each pitch of the example with its corresponding number. Transpose this example to the key of G. Number the pitches of the G scale 1-8. Using the new scale, transpose "Mary Had a Little Lamb." The first measure is done as an example.

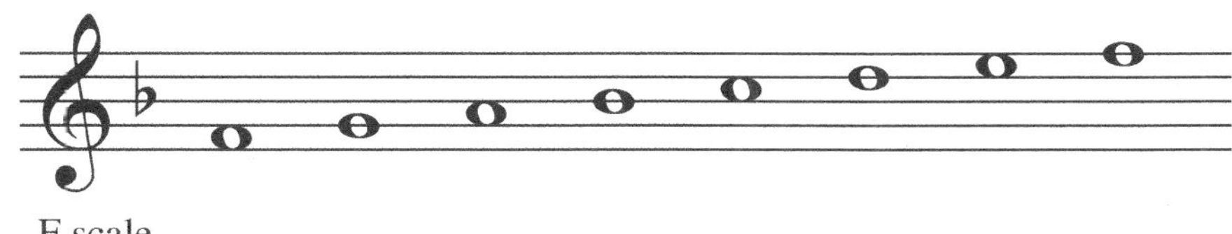

Mary Had a Little Lamb

Mary Had a Little Lamb

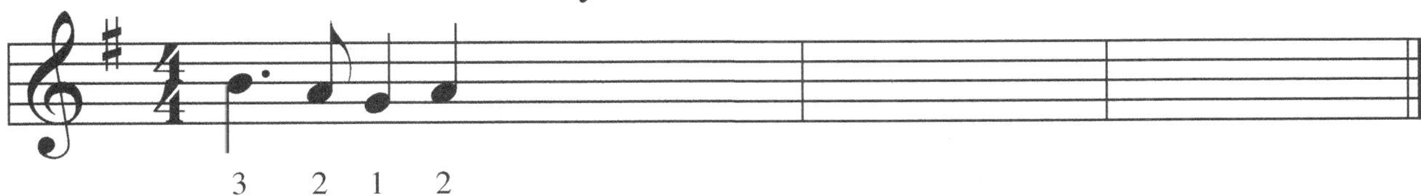

TRANSPOSE ANOTHER WAY!

"Lightly Row" is written in the key of D major. It begins on the 5th tone of the scale. Analyze the intervals between each pitch, labeling them under the example as shown.

Lightly Row

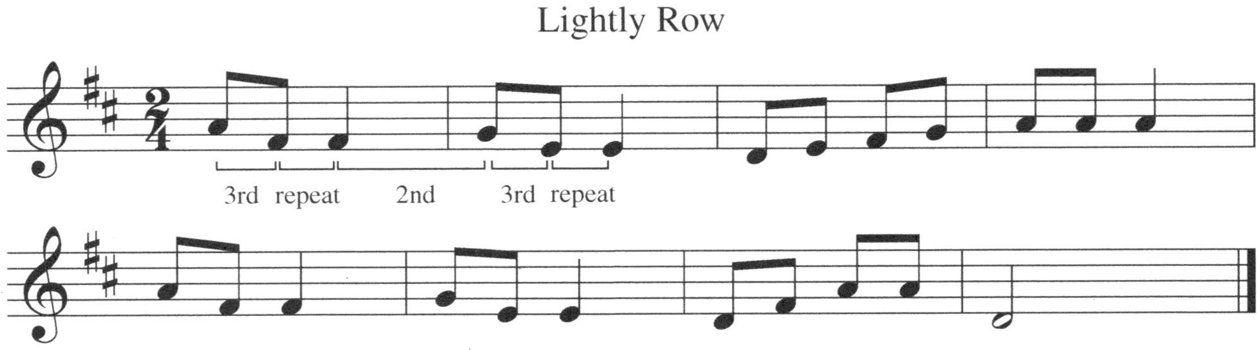

Now transpose "Lightly Row" to the key of C. Since this song begins on the 5th note of the scale, in the key of C, G is the 5th note. Transpose the example using the intervals you analyzed. The first measure is done for you.

Lightly Row

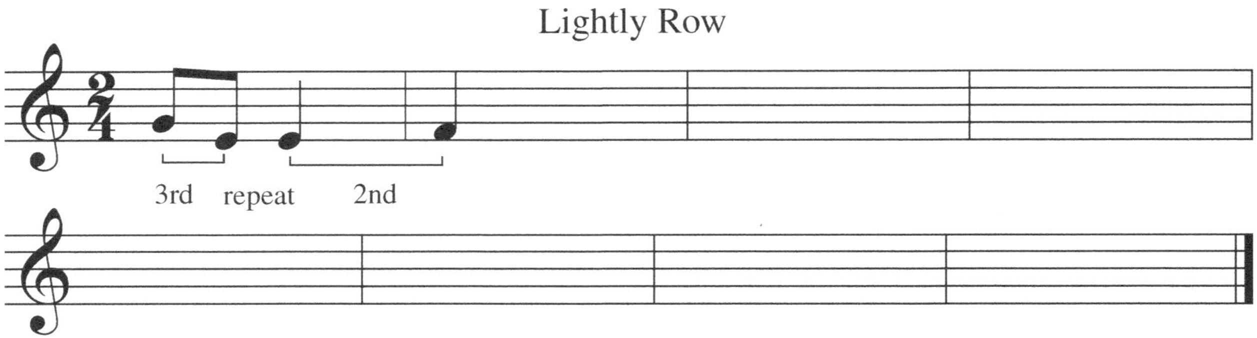

REFLECTION

Of the two ways to transpose, which did you find easiest? Why? Can you think of any other ways to transpose? Discuss your answers with the class.

____

____

____

____

____

TRANSCRIBING MUSIC

Name ______________________________

Have you ever heard a new tune on the radio and wished you could write it down so you could sing it again or play it on your instrument? Have you ever wanted to play a song with friends but didn't have a copy of the printed music? Learning to **transcribe** music, writing it down by listening to it or remembering it, is an important musical skill.

LEARN TO TRANSCRIBE

Fill in the missing notes in "Twinkle, Twinkle." Add the time signature. Hum along quietly if you need help. When you are finished, check your work on the piano or ask your teacher to take a look at it.

FIRST STEPS

The incomplete measures in "Yankee Doodle" contain repeated notes or notes that move up or down by step (2nds). Finish transcribing "Yankee Doodle."

DOWN ON THE FARM

The melody of "Old MacDonald Had a Farm" uses mostly stepwise movement (one note moving to the next in 2nds) and repeated notes. Using the notes given to get you started, finish transcribing "Old MacDonald." You may find it helpful to sing or hum the melody and tap the rhythm as you work. Exchange papers with a partner when you are finished to check each other's work.

PROJECT: CAN YOU HEAR IT?

There are 3 wrong pitches in "Row, Row, Row Your Boat." Can you find them? Circle the incorrect pitches and write in your corrections next to your circled notes.

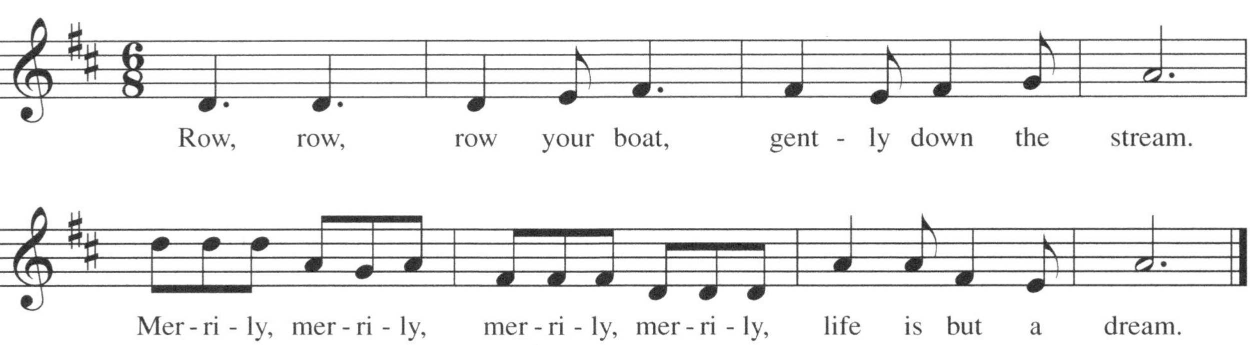

CHALLENGE

Working with a partner, practice transcribing rhythm patterns. While one partner taps, the other partner transcribes. Take turns. To continue this challenge, create new rhythm patterns on another sheet of paper.

COMPOSITION

Name _______________________________

Composing music means creating an original work with sound and rhythm. Composing music takes practice and a little patience. It can be an enjoyable and creative process.

COMPOSING RHYTHM

Add a rhythm to fit the words of the following riddle. Choose from the following note values and write your rhythm above the words.

Why do Birds fly south for the winter? Because it's too far to walk!

COMPOSING LYRICS

Add words, rhyming or not rhyming, serious or humorous, to the following rhythm pattern. Write the words under the notes.

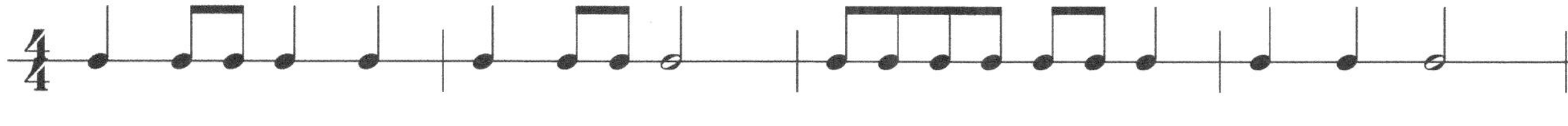

COMPOSING MELODY

Use the 5 notes given (they happen to be the first 5 notes of the C major scale) to create a melody using steps, skips or repeated notes. To begin, use only quarter notes, then as you create your melody, add other rhythms, if you like. Use the 1st and 2nd draft staves below to sketch and revise your work. Notate your finished melody on the last staff.

PROJECT: PUTTING IT TOGETHER

Choose riddle 1 or 2. Write a rhythm to fit the words. Compose a melody using the notes of the
D major scale. You may use some or all of the notes in the scale. Sketch out a rough draft, and
when you are satisfied with your work, title it and copy it on the bottom staff. Add a tempo indication, dynamics and articulation. Perform your finished composition for the class.

Riddle 1

Why did the chicken cross the road?
To get to the other side!

Riddle 2

What do you call a dog without a tail?
A hotdog!

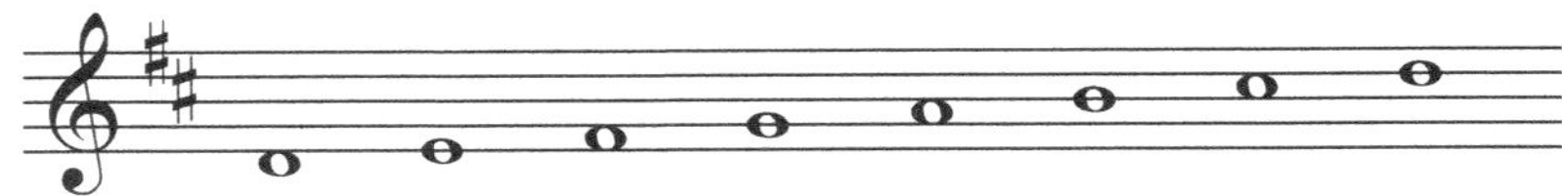

Draft Paper

Final Copy: ____

TEST YOUR MUSICAL KNOWLEDGE

Name ____

Name the treble and bass clef notes.

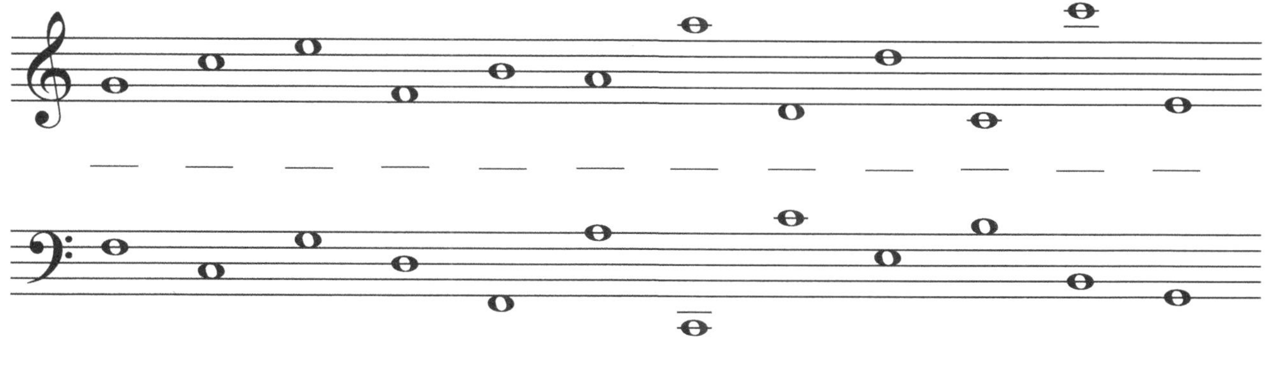

Add bar lines.

Fill in the top number of each time signature.

Notate the following melodic intervals. The first one is done for you.

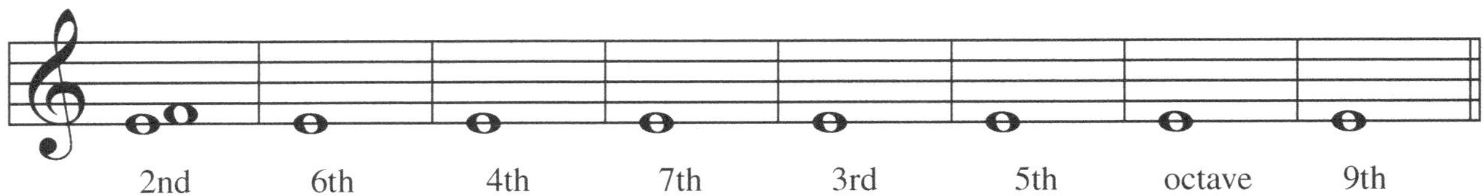

Mark the half and whole steps in the major and minor scale.

Name the triads by key name.

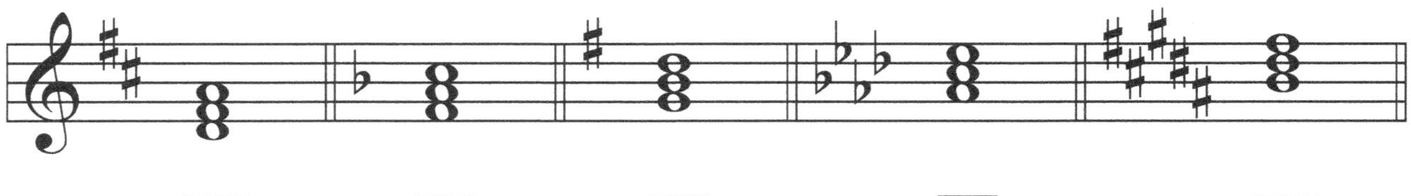

Find 8 mistakes in the music example. Circle each mistake.

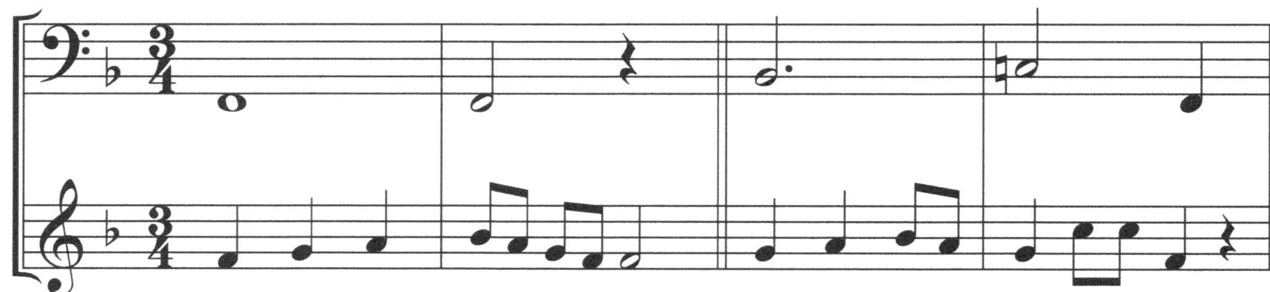

Transpose the following musical example to the key of C major.

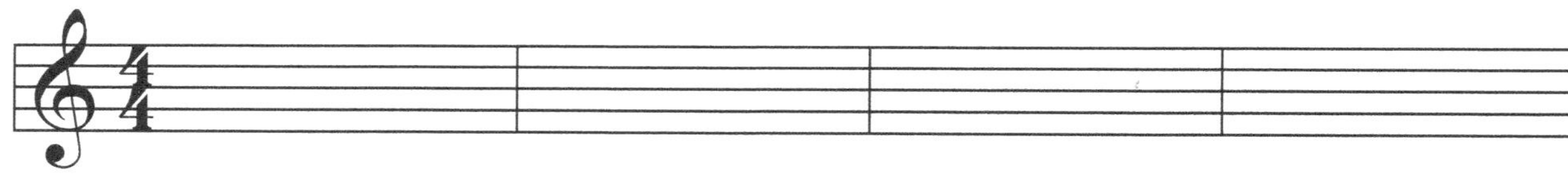

Match the musical terms with the correct definition.

accent	sharp, flat or natural not in the key signature
accidental	notes with different names that sound the same
beat	steady, recurring pulse
dot	silence in music
dynamics	added to a note it increases the value of the note
enharmonic	curved line connecting notes of the same pitch
flat	two numbers placed one above the other
key signature	short line that extends above or below the staff
ledger line	makes a pitch a half step higher
major scale	makes a pitch a half step lower
natural	cancels a sharp or flat
rest	sharps or flats to the right of the clef sign
sharp	set of pitches arranged WW H WWW H
slur	speed of the steady beat
staccato	symbols that show loudness or softness in music
tempo	short, detached
tie	smooth, connected
time signature	stressed sound
transposition	1st, 3rd and 5th notes of a scale played at the same time
triad	changing music from one key into another key

ANSWERS

SECTION 1: RHYTHM

LESSON 2, PAGE 5:
Music Math
1. T   2. F   3. T   4. T   5. F   6. F   7. T   8. F   9. F   10. F

LESSON 2, PAGE 6:
Fill in the blank.
1. 2   2. 4   3. 3   4. 2   5. 7   6. 3   7. 1   8. 7   9. 7   10. 10

LESSON 3, PAGE 7:
Rhythm Division

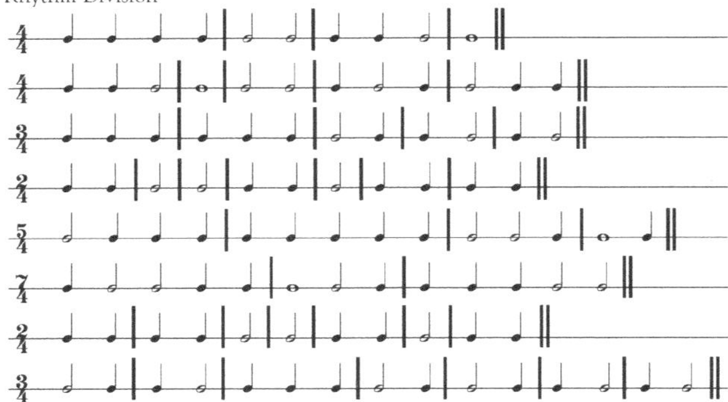

LESSON 3, PAGE 8:
Do You Have the Time?

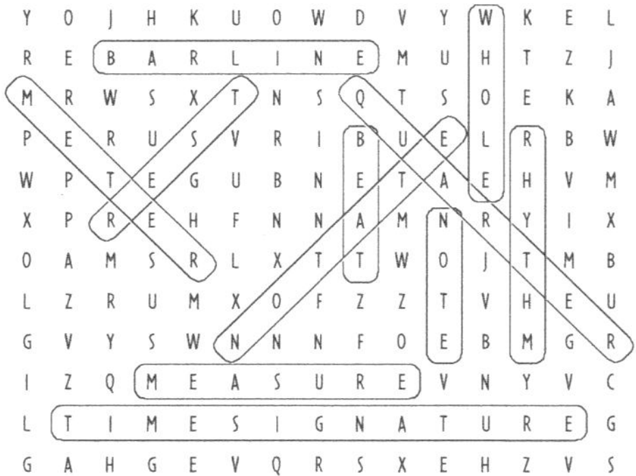

Rhythm Mania

LESSON 4, PAGE 9:
Rhythm Word Search

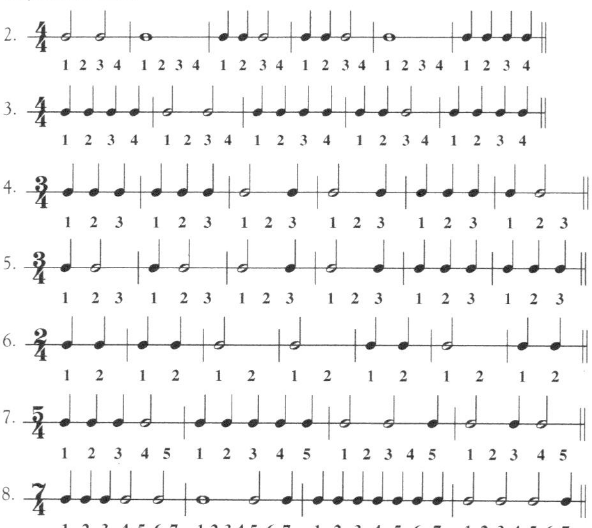

LESSON 4, PAGES 10-11:
Rhythms to Read

Project: You're the Maestro

$\frac{3}{4}$ My Country 'Tis of Thee

$\frac{2}{4}$ Jingle Bells

$\frac{4}{4}$ Frosty the Snowman

$\frac{4}{4}$ Mary Had a Little Lamb

$\frac{2}{4}$ Yankee Doodle

$\frac{4}{4}$ Go Tell Aunt Rhody

LESSON 5, PAGE 13:
Music Math
1. T   2. T   3. T   4. T   5. F   6. T   7. T   8. T   9. F   10. F

LESSON 5, PAGE 14:
Time for a Rest Review

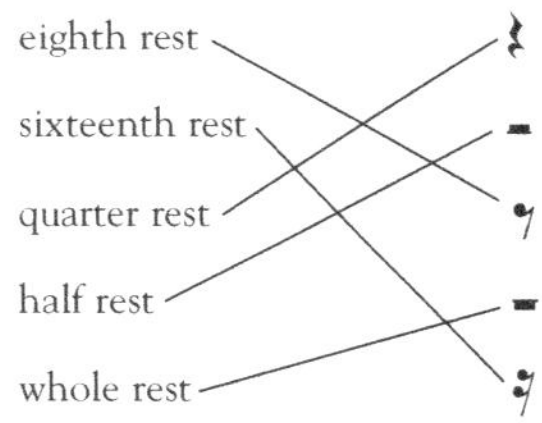

Project: Name Game

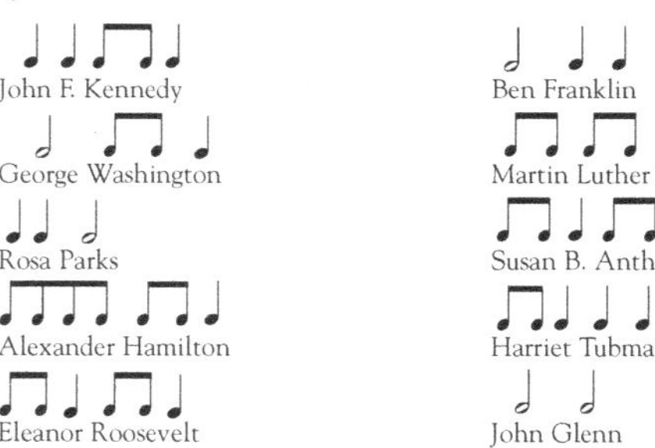

LESSON 6, PAGE 15:
Add a Dot

𝅘𝅥 = 1 beat	𝅘𝅥. = 1½ beats
𝅗𝅥 = 2 beats	𝅗𝅥. = 3 beats
𝅝 = 4 beats	𝅝. = 6 beats
𝅘𝅥𝅮 = ½ beat	𝅘𝅥𝅮. = ³/₄ beat
𝄽 = 1 beat	𝄽. = 1½ beats

LESSON 6, PAGE 16:
Time to Divide

Project: Find the Missing Dots

Challenge
1.   2.   3.   4.

LESSON 7, PAGE 17:
Who's Got the Beat?

Rhythm Relativity

LESSON 7, PAGE 18:
Rhythm Crossword

LESSON 8, PAGE 20:
Syncopation Challenge

LESSON 8, PAGE 21:
Project: Syncopation Aggravation

You're a grand old flag, you're a high fly - ing flag.

Oh Su - san-na, oh don't you cry for me.

I know a gal that I a - dore, Li'l Liz - a Jane.

How can I keep from sing-ing?

Some- bod - y's knock-ing at your door.

I got a mule, her name is Sal, fif-teen miles on the E-rie Can-al.

Joshua fit the battle of Jer-i - cho, Jer-i - cho, Jer-i - cho.

This lit-tle light of mine, I'm gon-na let it shine.

LESSON 9, PAGE 22:
A. True or False
1. T   2. T   3. F   4. F   5. F   6. T
7. F   8. F   9. F   10. T   11. T   12. F

B.

C. In 4/4 time:
1.   2.   3.   4.   5.   6.

In 6/8 time:
7.   8.   9.   10.   11.   12.

LESSON 9, PAGE 23:
D.

E.

SECTION 2: MELODY

LESSON 10, PAGE 24:
Line or Space?

LESSON 10, PAGE 25:
Project: Under Construction

LESSON 11, PAGE 26:
Test Yourself

LESSON 11, PAGE 27:
Musical Words

Keyboard Match

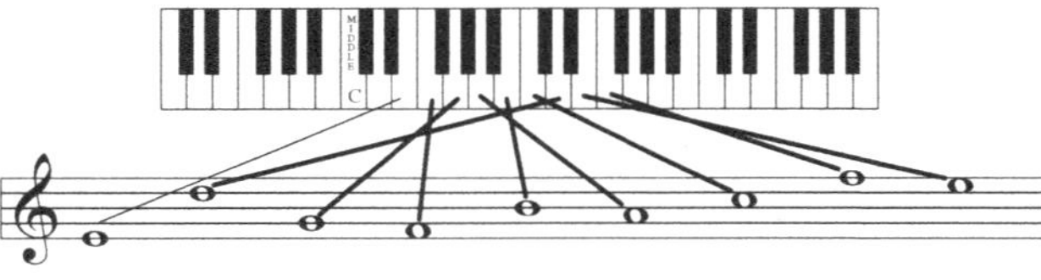

LESSON 12, PAGE 28:
Know the Bass Notes

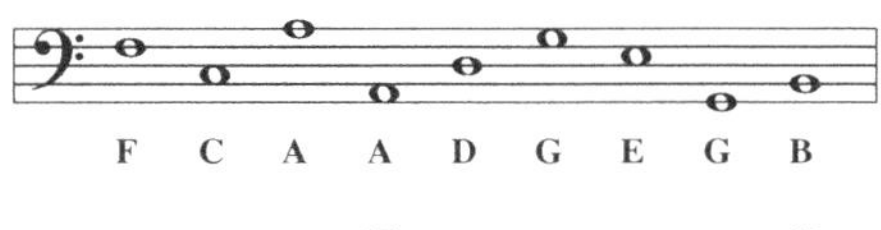

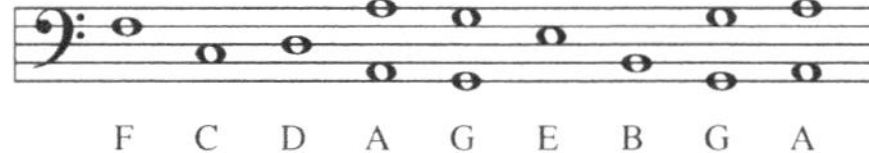

LESSON 12, PAGE 29:
Keyboard Match

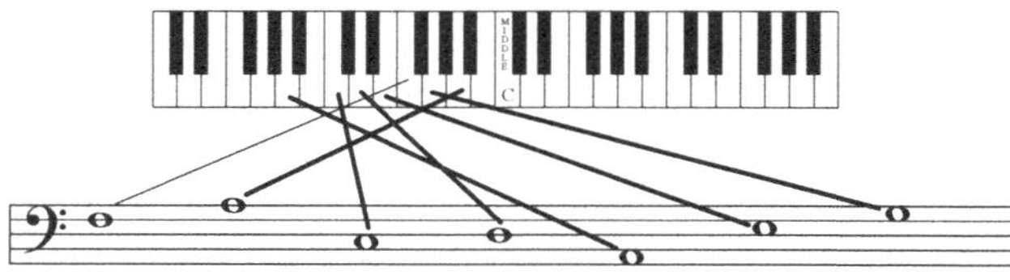

Spelling the Bass Clef

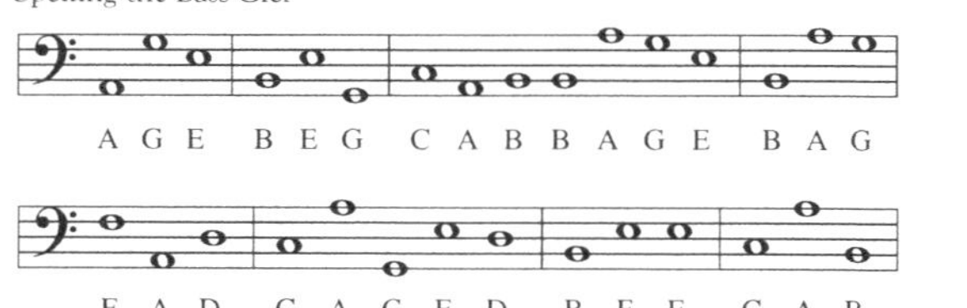

LESSON 12, PAGE 30:
Project: Clef Sleuth

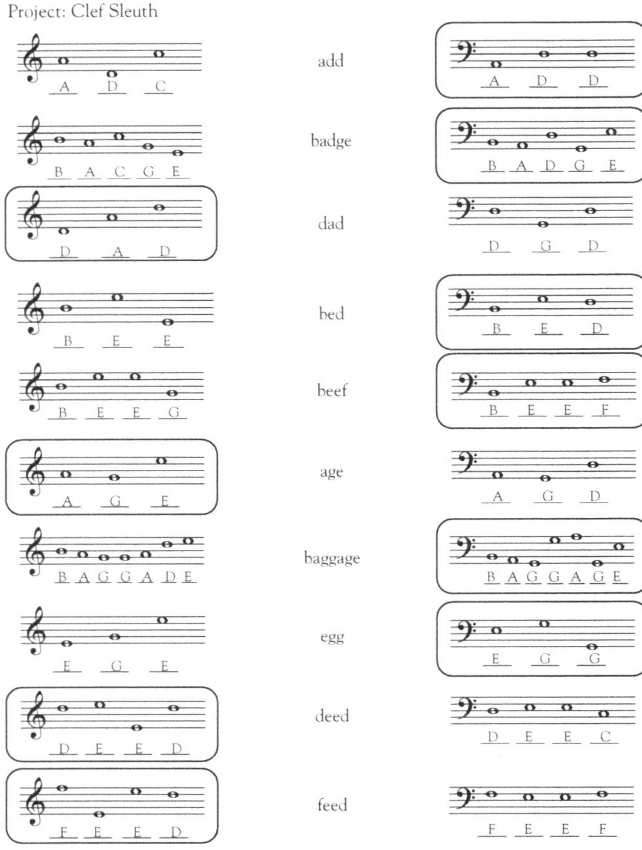

LESSON 13, PAGE 31:
Ledger Line Practice

Another Way to Write It

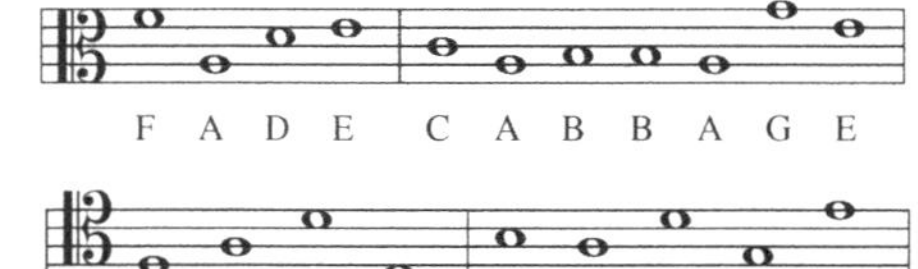

LESSON 13, PAGE 32:
Moveable Clef Challenge

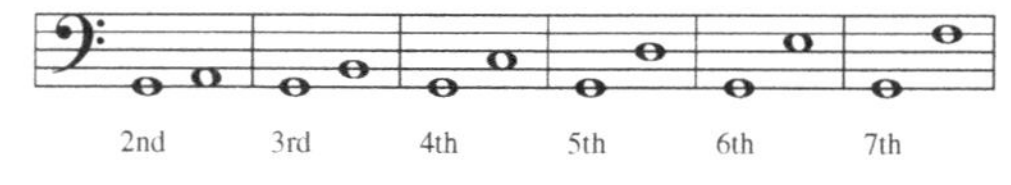

LESSON 14, PAGE 33:
Half or Whole?
1. W   2. H   3. H   4. W   5. H   6. W

LESSON 14, PAGE 35:
Project: Vocabulary Quiz
j   d   g   m   n   f   k   a   c   b   i   e   h   l

LESSON 15, PAGE 36:
Intervals

What's Your Interval?

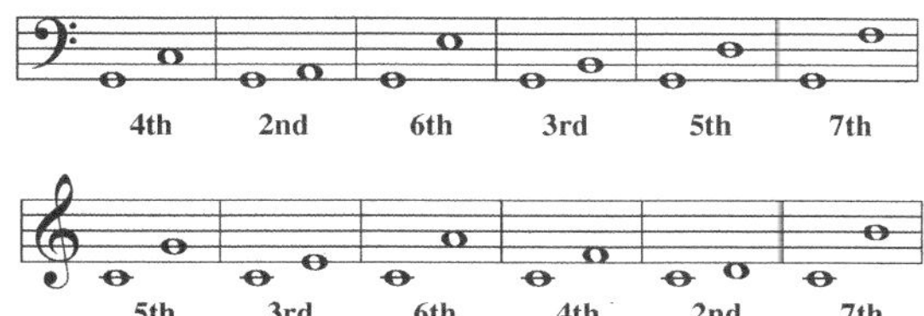

LESSON 15, PAGE 37:
Project: Interval Classification

	2nd	Harmonic	Simple
	5th	Harmonic	Simple
	octave	Melodic	Simple
	3rd	Harmonic	Simple
	4th	Harmonic	Simple
	octave	Melodic	Simple
	7th	Harmonic	Simple
	2nd	Melodic	Simple
	prime unison	Harmonic	Simple

LESSON 15, PAGE 38:
Challenge: Interval Dictation
Answers may vary. Here is one example of each interval in the treble clef.

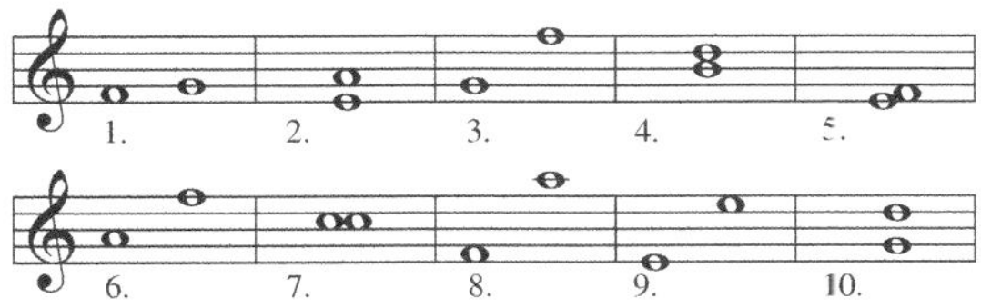

LESSON 16, PAGE 39:

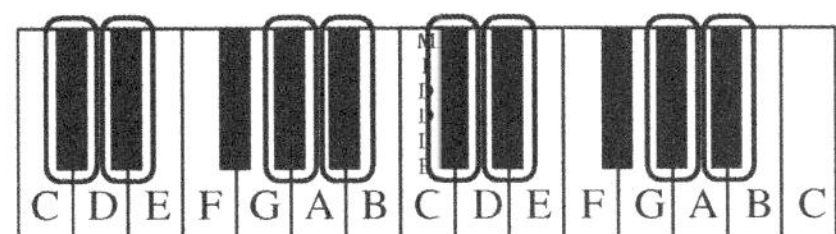

Sharps and Flats in the Treble Clef
1. F#, 2. Db, 3. Ab, 4. C#, 5. Eb, 6. D#, 7. Eb, 8. Bb, 9. F#, 10. G#

LESSON 16, PAGE 40:
Sharps and Flats in the Bass Clef
1. Ab, 2. D#, 3. G#, 4. Eb, 5. Gb, 6. Bb, 7. F#, 8. C#, 9. Bb

How Long?

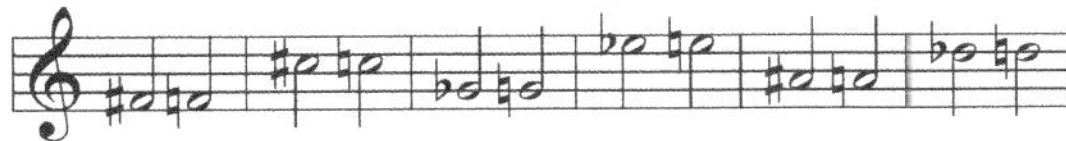

Project: Construction Zone

LESSON 17, PAGE 41:
Key Signature: Flats
Bb, Eb, Ab

Key Signature: Sharps
F#, C#

LESSON 17, PAGE 42:
Name That Sharp Key

LESSON 17, PAGE 43:
Name that Flat Key

Key of C

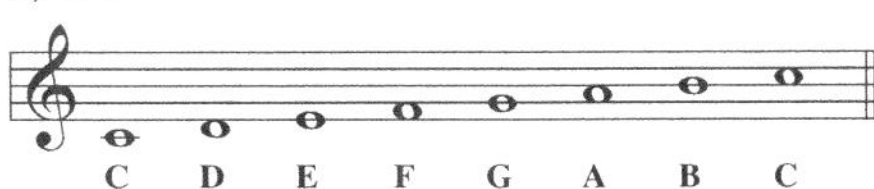

LESSON 17, PAGE 44:
Project: Key Match-Up

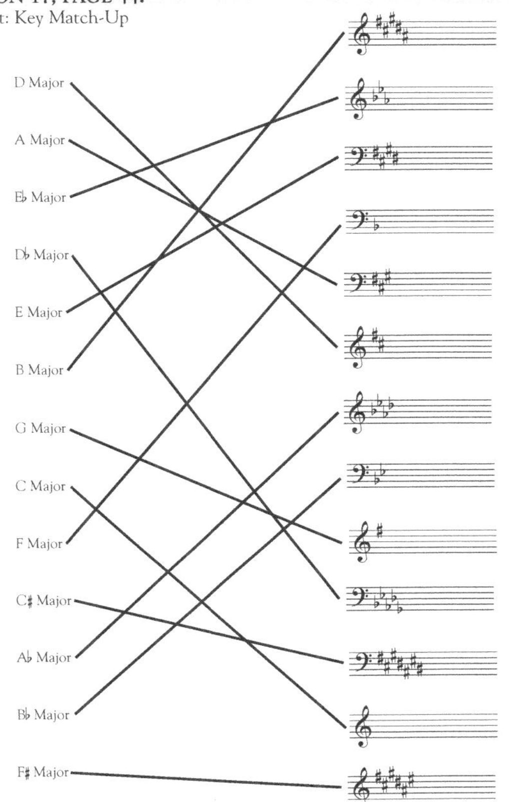

LESSON 18, PAGE 46:

Major or Minor?
1. C major
W W H W W W H H W W W H W W
2. A minor, harmonic
W H W H W H W+H H H W+H H W W H W
3. C minor, natural
W H W H W W W W H W W H W
4. E♭ major
W W H W W W H H W W W H W W
5. D minor, melodic
W H W W W W H W W H W W H W

Chromatic Scale

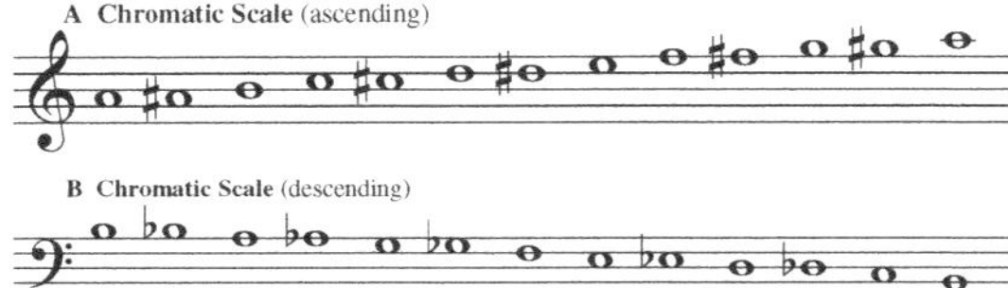

LESSON 18, PAGE 47:

Whole Tone Scale

Blues Scale

LESSON 19, PAGE 48:

Pitches on the Treble Staff
F D E C F A E G B

Pitches on the Bass Staff
F C G G E B A D A

Pitches on the Ledger Lines
A C B D E   C D C B A D

Mark an X on the keyboard.

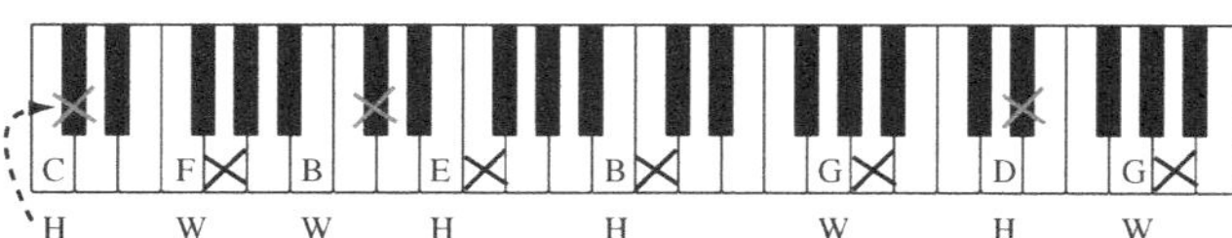

Melodic and Harmonic Intervals
H2nd, M5th, M3rd, M7th, M10th, M octave
H3rd, H5th, H4th, H6th, H unison, H7th, H5th

LESSON 19, PAGE 49:

M and H Intervals
Answers will vary. Here is one example of each.

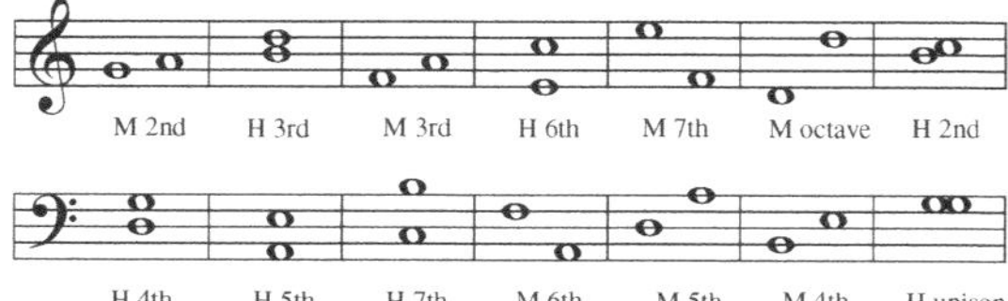

Major Key Signatures

True or False?
T, F, T, F, T, F, T

SECTION 3: TOOL BOX

LESSON 20, PAGE 50:

Time for a Change
B♮, A♮, E♮, B♮, F♮

Name these enharmonic notes.

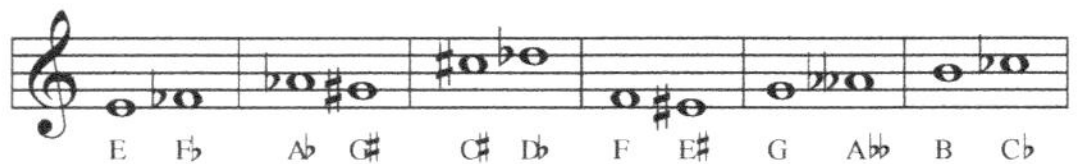

LESSON 20, PAGE 51:

Enharmonic Notation

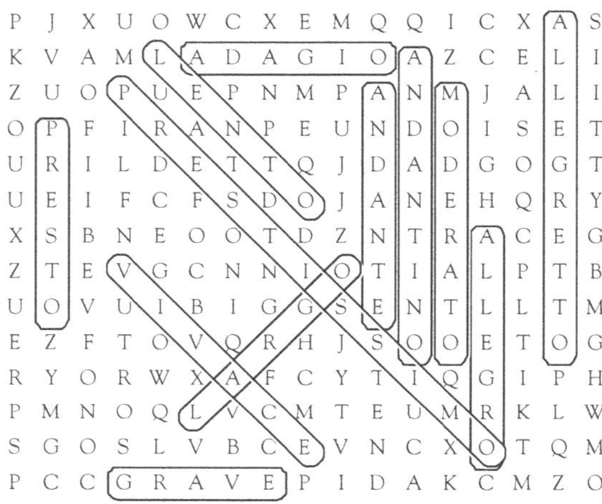

Project: Ask the Composer
1. Key of D; F and C;   2. Yes;   3. F double sharp;   4. A♯; black key
5. G♯; 6. No; 7. No;   8. E♭, Yes;   9. to cancel previous C♯; 10. E♭

LESSON 21, PAGE 52:

Tempo Word Search

<pre>
P J X U O W C X E M Q Q I C X A S
K V A M L A D A G I O A Z C E L I
Z U O P U E P N M P A N M J A L I
O P F I R A N P E U N D O I S E T
U R I L D E T T Q J D A D G O G T
U E I F C F S D O J A N E H Q R Y
X S B N E O O T D Z N T R A C E G
Z T E V G C N N I O T I A L P T O
U O V U I B I G G S E N T L L T O
E Z F T O V Q R H J S O E T O T G
R Y O R W X A F C Y T I Q G I P H
P M N O Q L V C M T E U M R K L W
S G O S L V B C E V N C X O T Q M
P C C G R A V E P I D A K C M Z O
</pre>

LESSON 21, PAGE 53:

Tempo Translation
molto vivace – very lively
allegro non troppo – not too fast
acccelerando poco a poco – increase tempo little by little
molto ritardando – decrease tempo very much

Project: Choose the Tempo
Answers will vary. Here are suggested tempo markings.
1. Oh, Susanna – Moderato
2. America the Beautiful – Andante
3. Chopsticks – Presto
4. This Land Is Your Land – Allegro
5. When the Saints Go Marching In – Vivace

LESSON 22, PAGE 54:

Italian Scramble
apino = piano; rftoe = forte; simpsioina = pianissimo; mezoz nopai = mezzo piano
edonccsre = crescendo; ocdrseeecnd = decrescendo; smifirotos = fortissimo

LESSON 23, PAGE 56:

Articulation Crossword

Slur or Tie?

LESSON 23, PAGE 57:
Project: What's Your Style?

Row, Row, Row Your Boat

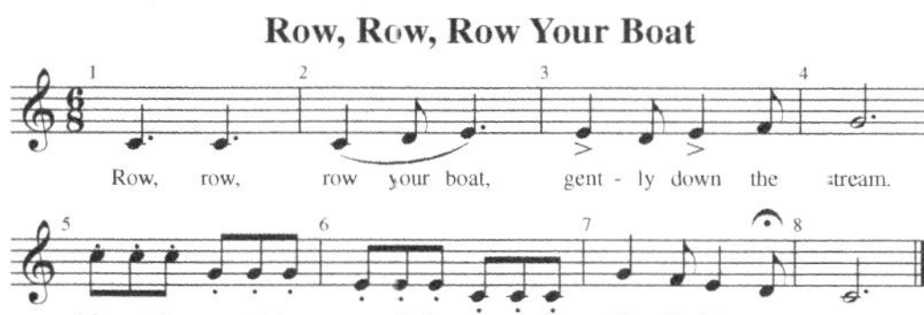

LESSON 24, PAGE 58:
Form Identification

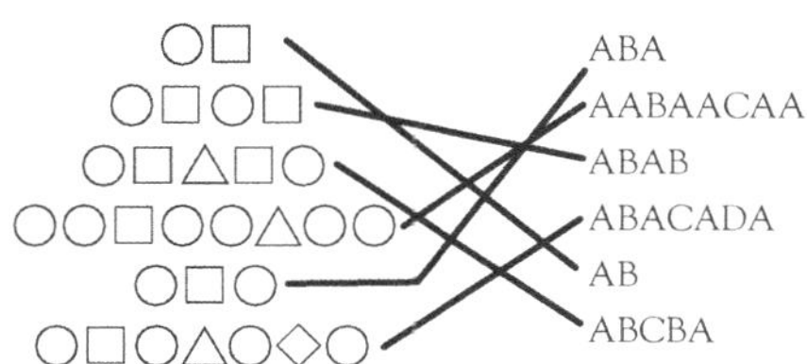

LESSON 24, PAGE 59:
Form Detail

Project: Formulations

$\frac{4}{4}$ A B A'; $\frac{2}{4}$ A B A C; $\frac{3}{4}$ A B A' B'; $\frac{6}{8}$ A B A E' A'

LESSON 25, PAGE 61:
Which Way Do I Go?

LESSON 25, PAGE 62:
Which Way Do I Go? (cont.)

LESSON 26, PAGE 63:
Time for Tonic

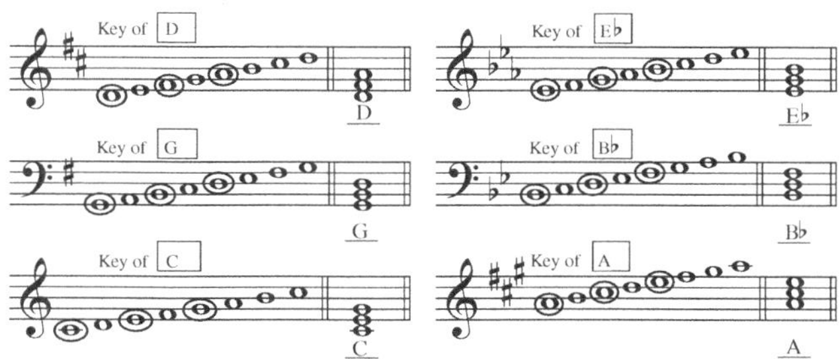

LESSON 26, PAGE 64:
Dominant Triads

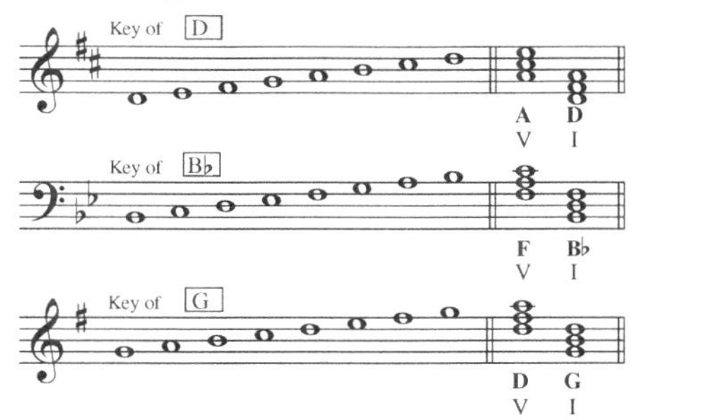

Project: Cadence Detective

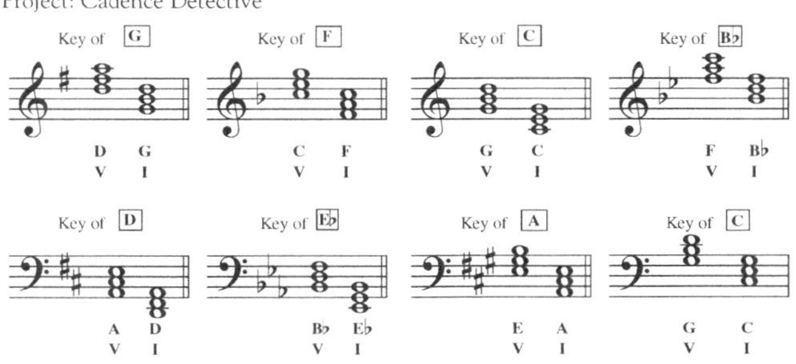

LESSON 27, PAGE 65:
Time to Transpose!

LESSON 27, PAGE 66:
Transpose Another Way!

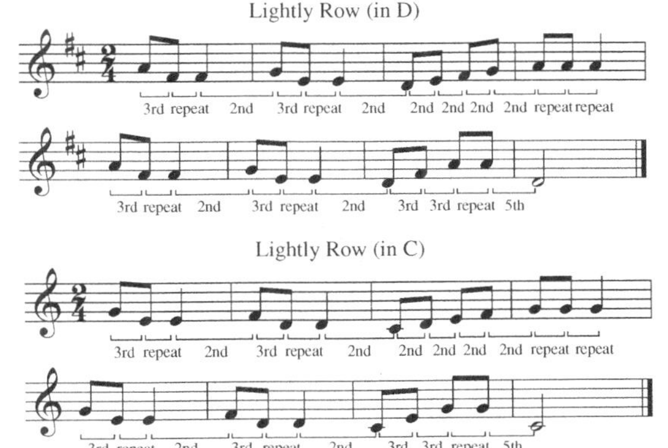

LESSON 28, PAGE 67:
Learn to Transcribe

First Steps

LESSON 28, PAGE 68:
Down on the Farm

Project: Can You Hear It?

LESSON 30, PAGE 71:
Treble and Bass Clef Notes

Barlines

Time Signature

LESSON 30, PAGE 72:
Melodic Intervals

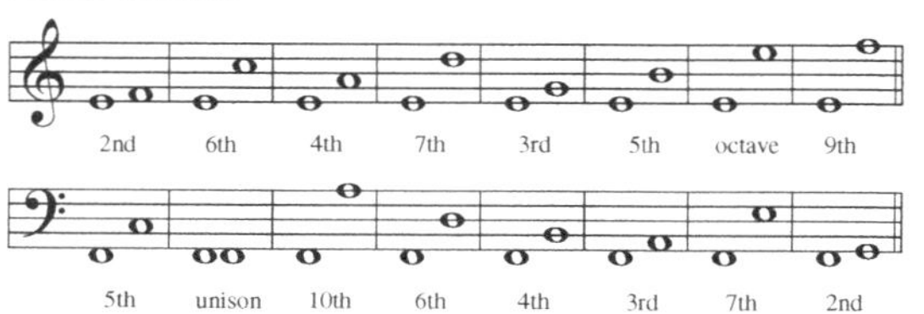

F Major Scale

LESSON 30, PAGE 73:

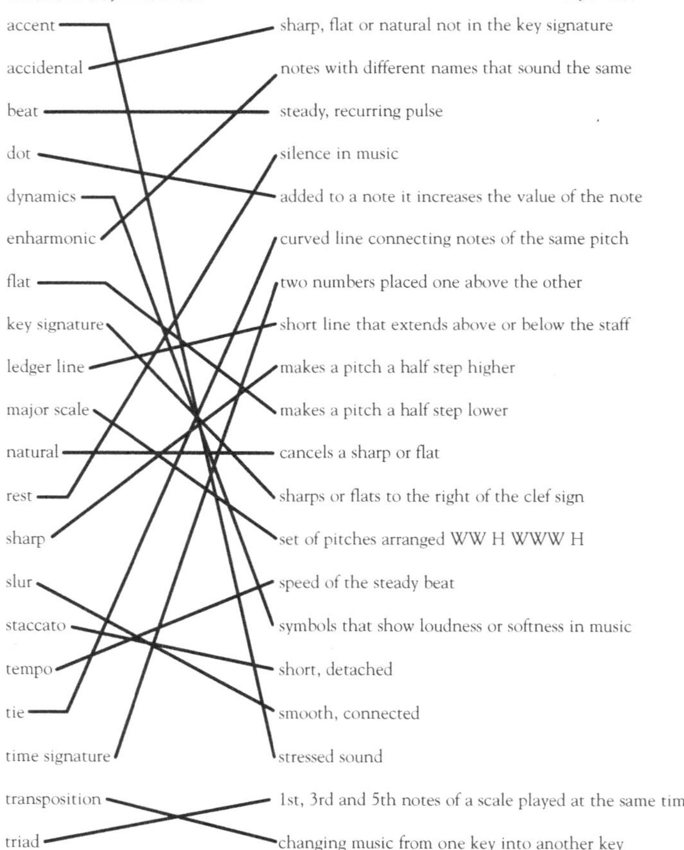